Lincoln Hall

Songs of sovereign grace

For use in all religious gatherings

Lincoln Hall

Songs of sovereign grace
For use in all religious gatherings

ISBN/EAN: 9783337266288

Printed in Europe, USA, Canada, Australia, Japan

Cover: Foto ©Lupo / pixelio.de

More available books at **www.hansebooks.com**

SONGS OF
SOVEREIGN GRACE,

.....FOR USE IN ALL.....

RELIGIOUS GATHERINGS

.....BY.....

J. LINCOLN HALL

✷ WILLIAM J. KIRKPATRICK ✷

W. S. WEEDEN

HALL-MACK CO.
PUBLILHERS

416 ARCH STREET.   -   -   -   PHILADELPHIA

COPYRIGHTED 1897, BY HALL-MACK CO.

....PREFACE....

In presenting SONGS OF SOVEREIGN GRACE to the hosts of Christian workers, we believe we are giving them a book which is adapted to every form of Evangelical work.

The editors have, for years, been engaged in spreading the gospel of our Lord and Saviour, Jesus Christ, through the medium of sacred songs, and they feel that they are especially qualified for the responsible work into which they have entered.

No expense or care has been spared in making Songs of Sovereign Grace the best book ever presented to the Christian public; we trust the cause of Christ may be advanced through our efforts.

Yours in Christian Song,

J. LINOLN HALL,
WILLIAM J. KIRKPATRICK,
W. S. WEEDEN.

Songs of Sovereign Grace.

SOVEREIGN GRACE.

IRVIN H. MACK. J. LINCOLN HALL.

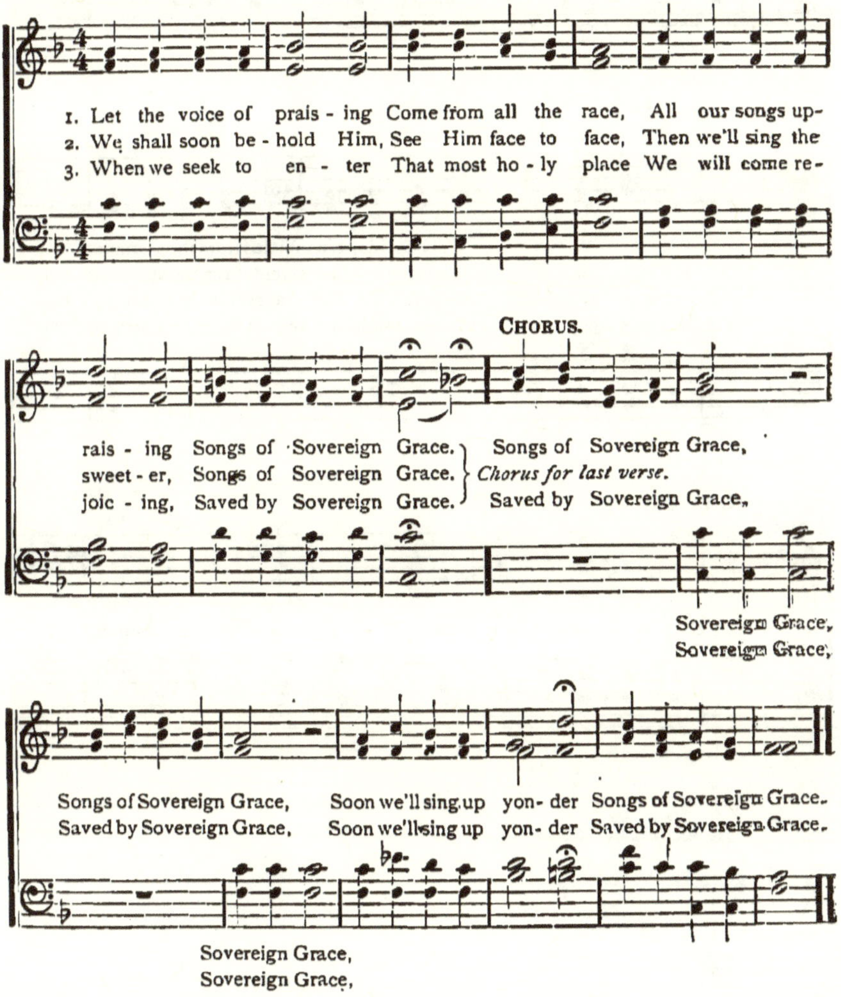

1. Let the voice of prais-ing Come from all the race, All our songs up-
2. We shall soon be-hold Him, See Him face to face, Then we'll sing the
3. When we seek to en-ter That most ho-ly place We will come re-

CHORUS.

rais - ing Songs of Sovereign Grace. ⎫ Songs of Sovereign Grace,
sweet - er, Songs of Sovereign Grace. ⎬ *Chorus for last verse.*
joic - ing, Saved by Sovereign Grace. ⎭ Saved by Sovereign Grace,

Sovereign Grace,
Sovereign Grace,

Songs of Sovereign Grace, Soon we'll sing up yon - der Songs of Sovereign Grace.
Saved by Sovereign Grace, Soon we'll sing up yon - der Saved by Sovereign Grace.

Sovereign Grace,
Sovereign Grace,

4 HE SHIELDS FROM THE STORMS OF LIFE.

E. C. MACARTNEY. W. S. WEEDEN.

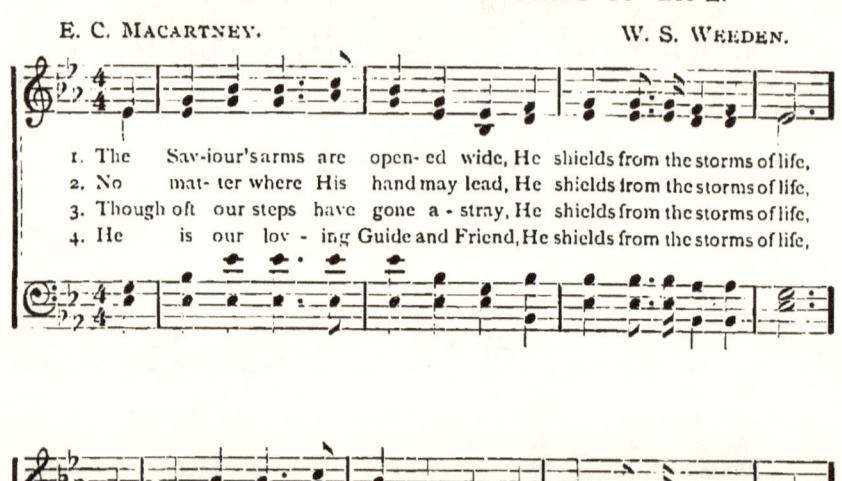

1. The Saviour's arms are open-ed wide, He shields from the storms of life,
2. No mat-ter where His hand may lead, He shields from the storms of life,
3. Though oft our steps have gone a-stray, He shields from the storms of life,
4. He is our lov-ing Guide and Friend, He shields from the storms of life,

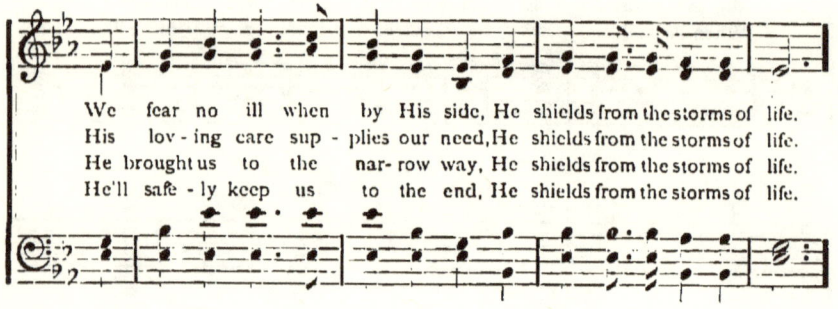

We fear no ill when by His side, He shields from the storms of life.
His lov-ing care sup-plies our need, He shields from the storms of life.
He brought us to the nar-row way, He shields from the storms of life.
He'll safe-ly keep us to the end, He shields from the storms of life.

CHORUS.

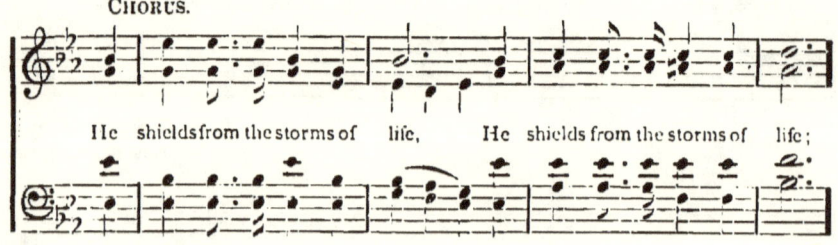

He shields from the storms of life, He shields from the storms of life;

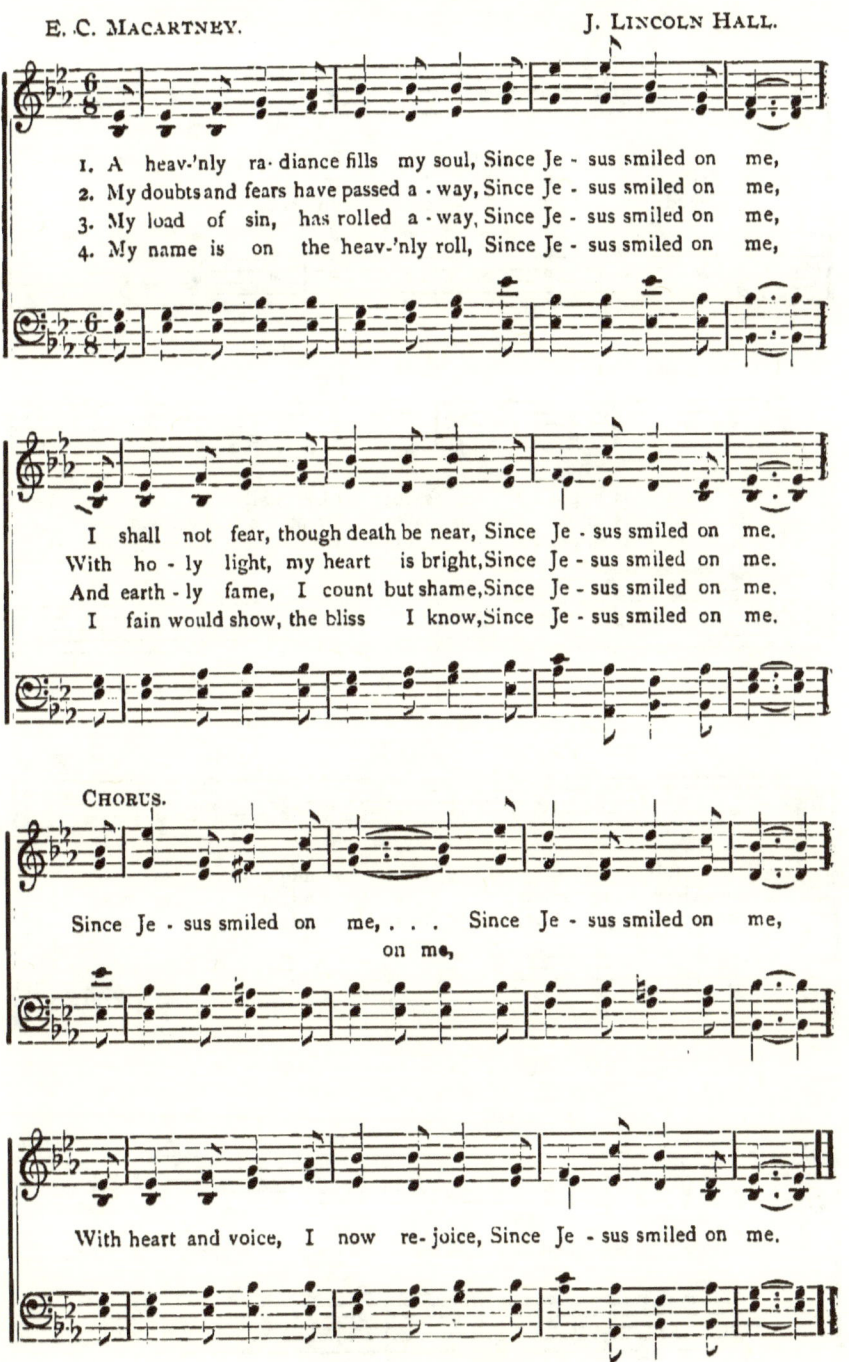

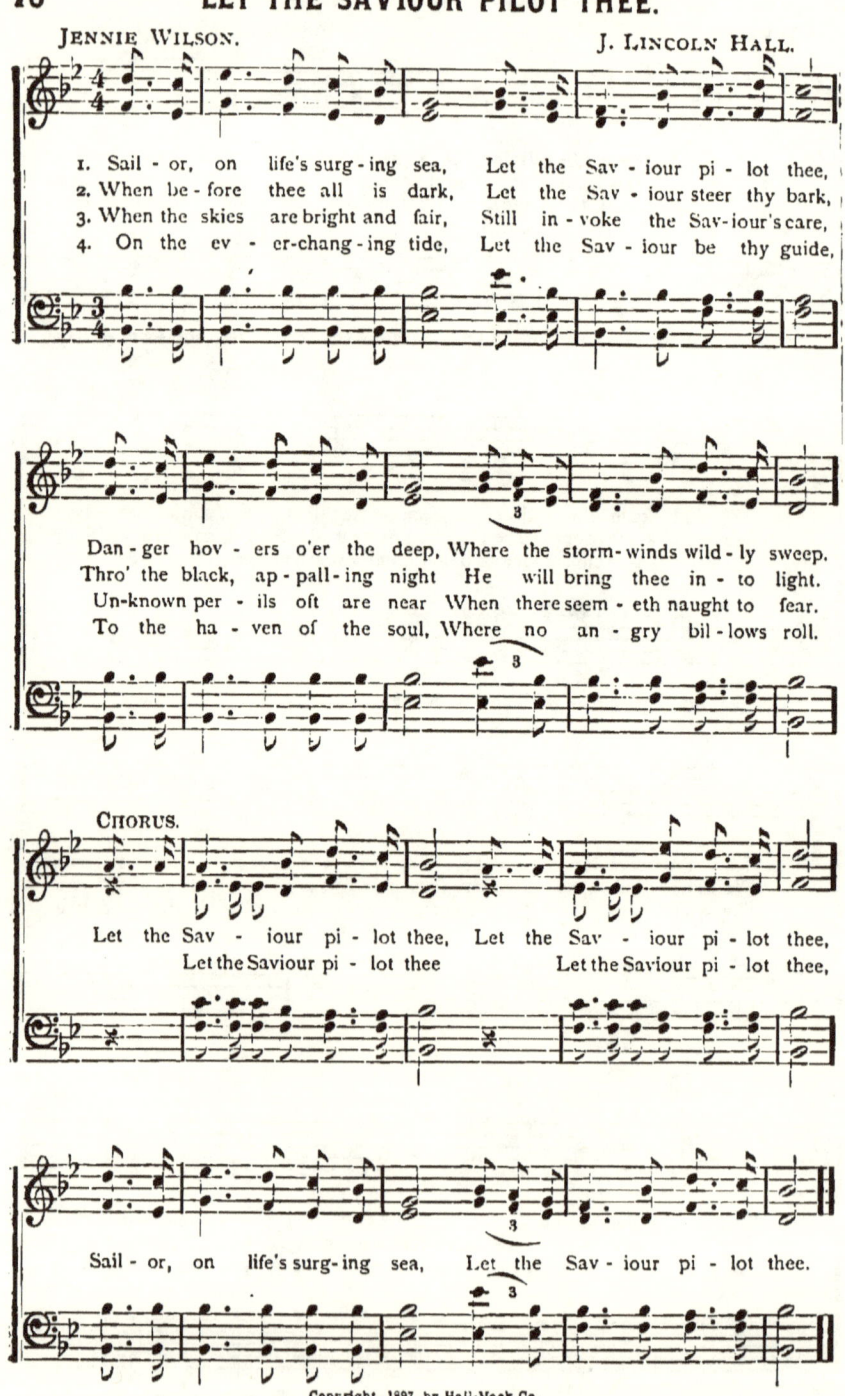

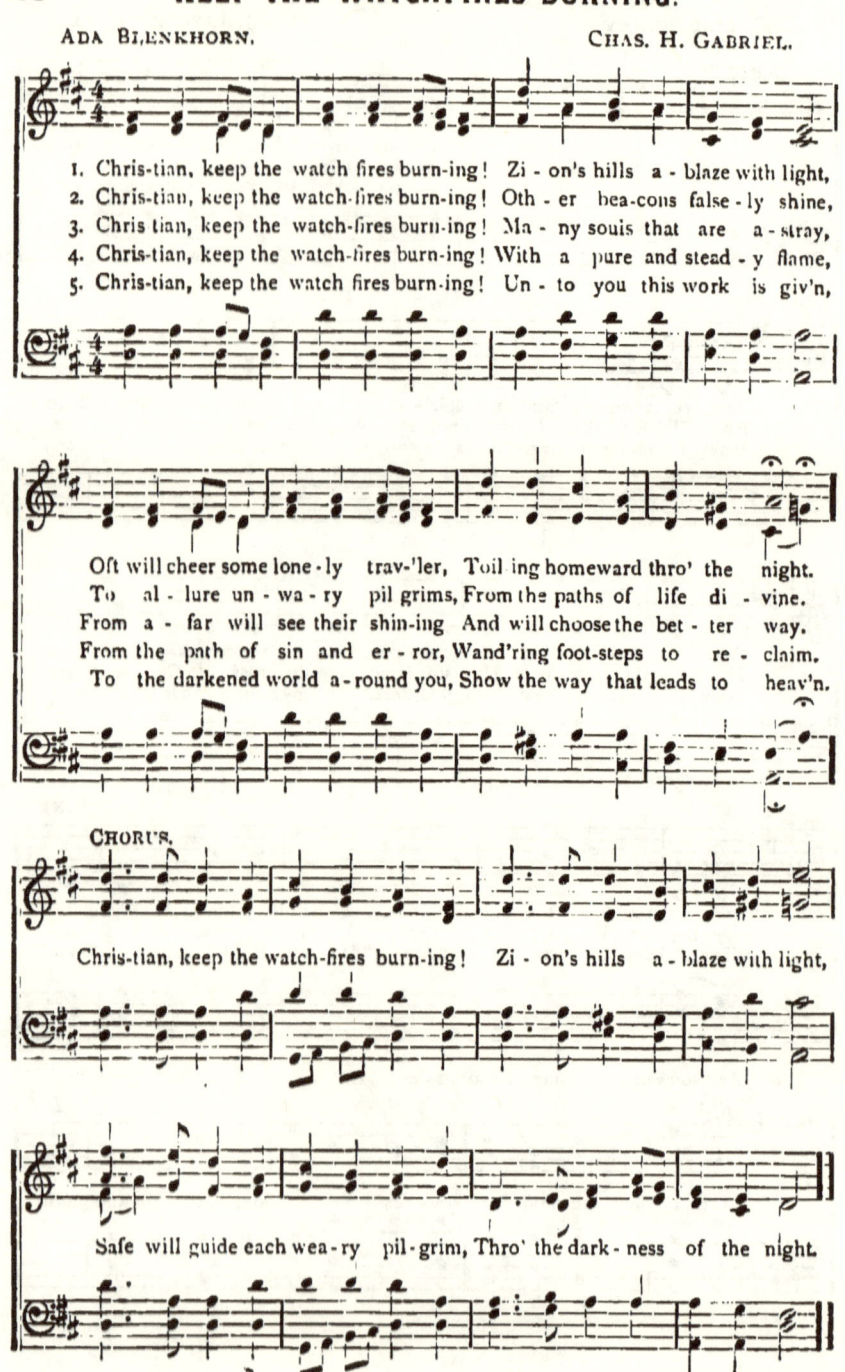

THE SHADOW OF THE ROCK.

Mrs. ANNIE E. THOMPSON. FRANK M. DAVIS, by per.

1. In a wea-ry land I wan-der, And with falt-'ring steps I walk;
2. Here my toils are un-a-bat-ing, And rude cares a-bout me mock;
3. In these pas-tures fair and ver-nal, With my Shep-herd's cho-sen flock
4. By these wa-ters gen-tly flow-ing, I shall fear no tem-pest's shock,
5. So with pa-tient faith I'll wan-der, And with lov-ing trust will walk,

But I soon shall rest up yon-der In the shad-ow of the Rock.
But my rest is yon-der wait-ing In the shad-ow of the Rock.
I shall feast on joys e-ter-nal In the shad-ow of the Rock.
And no want or grief be know-ing In the shad-ow of the Rock.
For I'll soon be rest-ing yon-der In the shad-ow of the Rock.

CHORUS.

In the shad-ow of the Rock, In the shad-ow of the Rock,
I will soon be rest-ing yon-der In the shad-ow of the Rock.

22. COMING TO THE CROSS OF JESUS.

JENNIE WILSON. J. LINCOLN HALL.

1. Burdened with my guilt and shame, With no mer-it I can claim, Call-ing on the sav-ing name,
2. Wea-ry of the way of sin, Filled with doubts and fears within, Longing par-don's peace to win,
3. Ut-ter help-less-ness to plead, Trusting Him who knows my need, My re-pen-tant pray'r will heed,
4. Clinging to the prom-ise blest, That the sad and guilt-op-pressed Here may find sweet joy and rest,

I am coming to the cross of Je - sus.

CHORUS.

I am com-ing to the cross, Counting world-ly pleas-ures dross, I am com-ing, I am coming to the cross; At the dear Re-deemer's feet, I will find sal-va-tion sweet, I am coming, I am coming to the cross.

Copyright, 1897, by Hall-Mack Co.

GLAD ALL THE DAY.—Concluded. 31

round our way We can see His love shin-ing ev - 'ry where.
We can see the Father's love so brightly shining ev 'ry where.

And we praise Him that He makes the world so bright and fair.

MAKE ME MORE LIKE JESUS.

Mrs. M. E. Baldwin. Adam Geibel.

1. Heav'nly Fa - ther, this I pray, Make me more like Je - sus;
2. Fa - ther, teach me day by day, To be more like Je - sus!
3. In sub - mis-sion, faith, and love, Make me more like Je - sus!

FINE.

Lead me in the heav'n-ly way, Make me more like Je - sus.
Teach me how to watch and pray, And be more like Je - sus.
Grant this bless-ing from a - bove, Make me more like Je - sus.

D.S.—Lead me in the heav'n-ly way, Make me more like Je - sus.

CHORUS. D.S.

More and more, more and more, More and more like Je - sus;

Copyright, 1897, by Wm. J. Kirkpatrick.

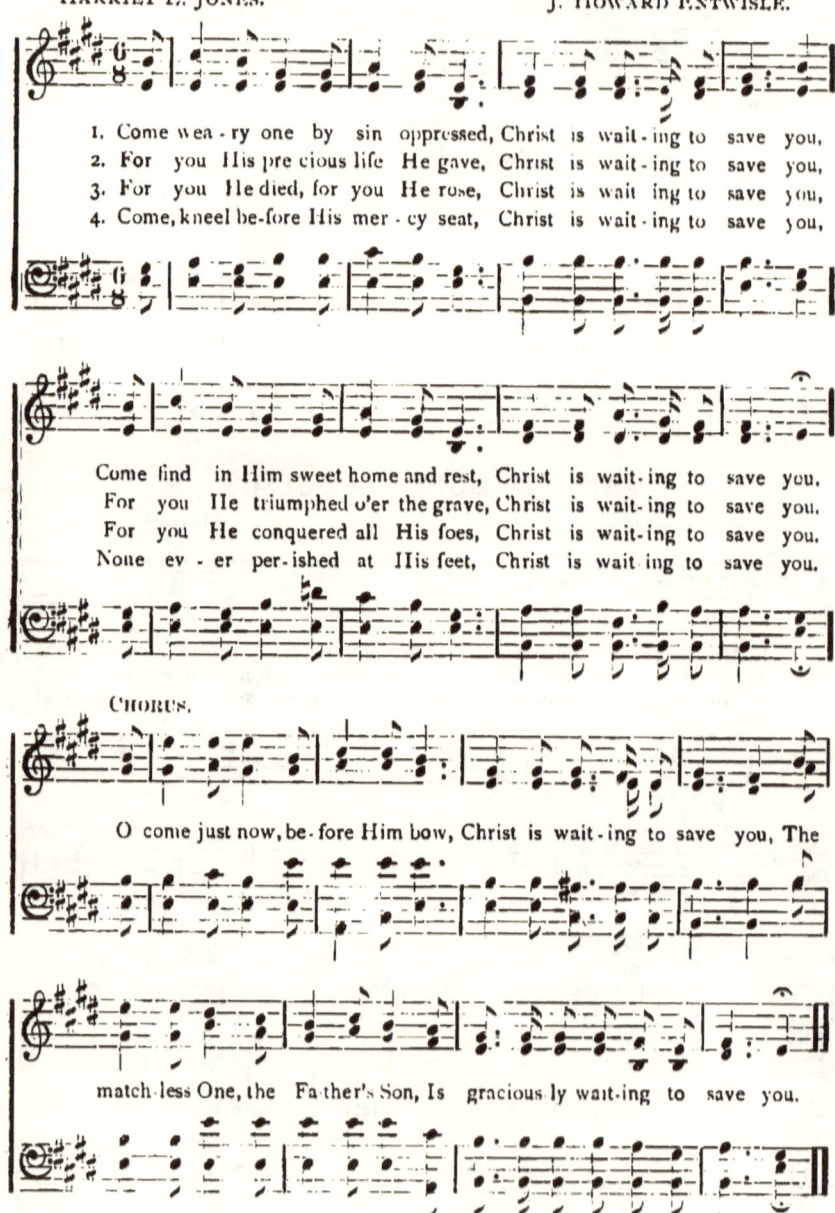

34 WALKING IN THE SUNLIGHT.

BIRDIE BELL.
A. J. SHOWALTER, by per.
On board S. S. "Berlin," July 1, 1895.

1. Walk-ing in the sun-light, on I go each day, Trav-'ling to a
2. Walk-ing in the sun-light of a Fa-ther's love, Press-ing on with
3. Walk-ing in the sun-light, close by Je-sus' side, Fear-ing naught, I
4. Walk-ing in the sun-light till I catch a sight Of the Cit-y's

land be-yond com-pare; Sing-ing of God's mercies all a long the way,
swift and will-ing feet; Rest e-ter-nal waits me in that land a-bove,
jour-ney on the way; In my weakness clinging to my trust-y Guide,
pearl-y gates a-bove; Je-sus' pres ence scatters darkest shades of night,

REFRAIN.

Walk-ing in the sun-light bright and fair.
Walk-ing in the sun light glad and sweet.
Walk-ing in the sun light, day by day.
Walk-ing in the sun light of God's love.
} Walking in the sun-light,

bless-ed light of God, Sing-ing of His mercies' ceaseless flow, Foll'wing in the

path-way which my Lord hath trod, Walking in the sun-light, on I go.

Copyright, 1896, by A. J. Showalter.

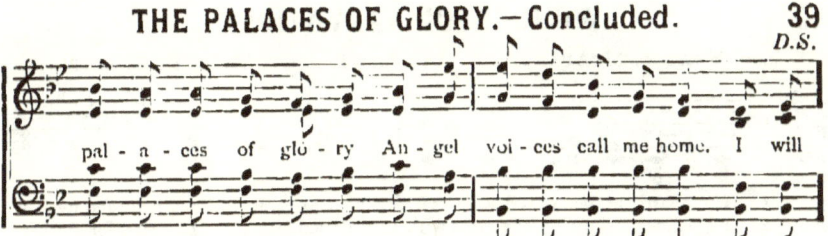

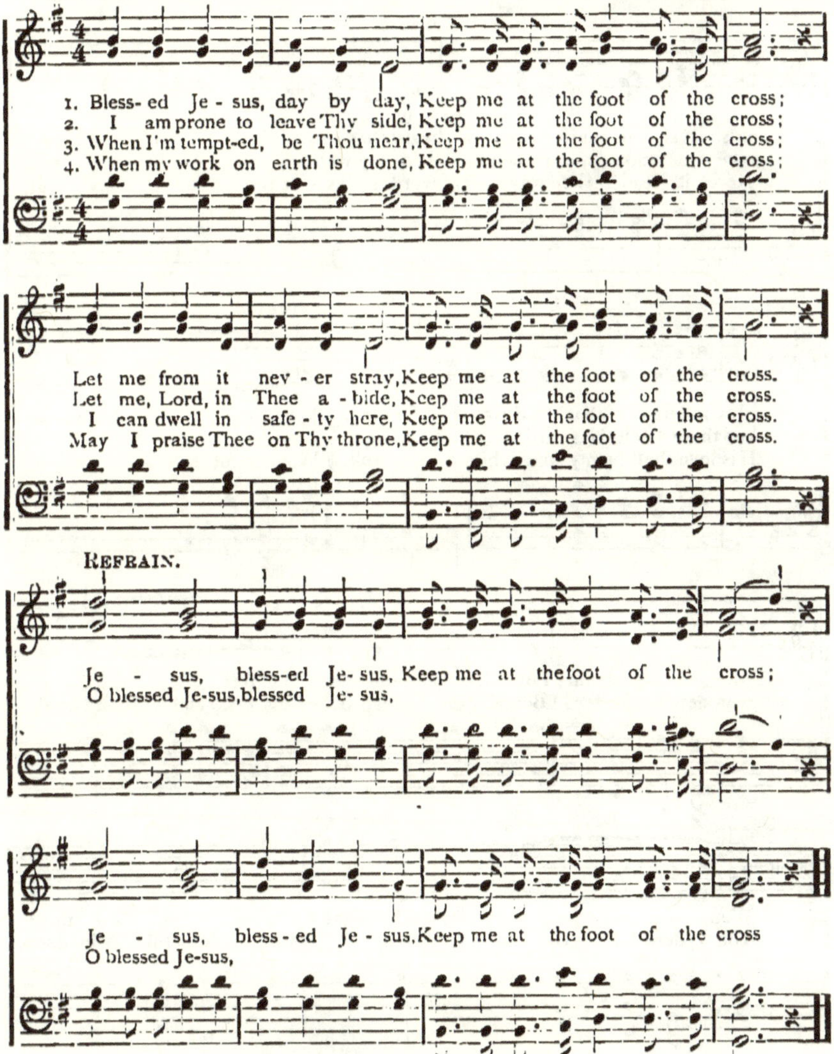

40. WONDERFUL SALVATION.

Rev. NEAL A. MCAULAY.   CHAS. H. GABRIEL.

1. I heard the bless-ed song of God's free grace, How poor and need-y souls His love could trace; I heard that Je-sus bled up on the tree,—I wondered if that blood was shed for me.
2. I came un-to the cross with bur-dened soul, I cried for cleaning grace to make me whole; I laid my wea-ry heart at Je-sus' feet, And there I felt His pard'ning love so sweet.
3. And now I love to work for Him each day, 'Tis sweet to have His spir-it lead the way, His word is ev-er pre-cious to my soul, His love shall be my song while a-ges roll.

CHORUS.

Won - - - der-ful sal-va - - - tion! Boundless, deep and wide and so free, ...
Wonder-ful sal-va-tion, won-der-ful in-deed! Bound-less, deep boundless, deep and wide and free!

Won - - - - der-ful sal-va - - - tion:
Won-der-ful sal-va-tion, won-der-ful in-deed,

Copyright, 1897, by Hull-Mauk Co.

WONDERFUL SALVATION.—Concluded. 41

Pur-chased by His death up-on the tree........
Pur - chased by His death up-on the tree.

WE MARCH TO VICTORY.

JENNIE MORTON. HOWARD CLARE.

1. { We march be-neath the ban-ner of the King, And as we march we
   { Let all u-nite and make the cho-rus ring, (*Omit*........
2. { We march, we march with courage firm and strong, The tri umph will by
   { Come with us then and join our hap-py song, (*Omit*........

glad-ly, gladly sing; We march to vic-to-ry. }
faith to us be-long; We march to vic-to-ry. }

CHORUS.

Then a way, a-way, hear the call to-day And the bat-tle is be-fore us, Yet we nev-er fear, for Christ our help is near, And His eye is al-ways o'er us.

Copyright, 1895, by Hall-Mack Co.

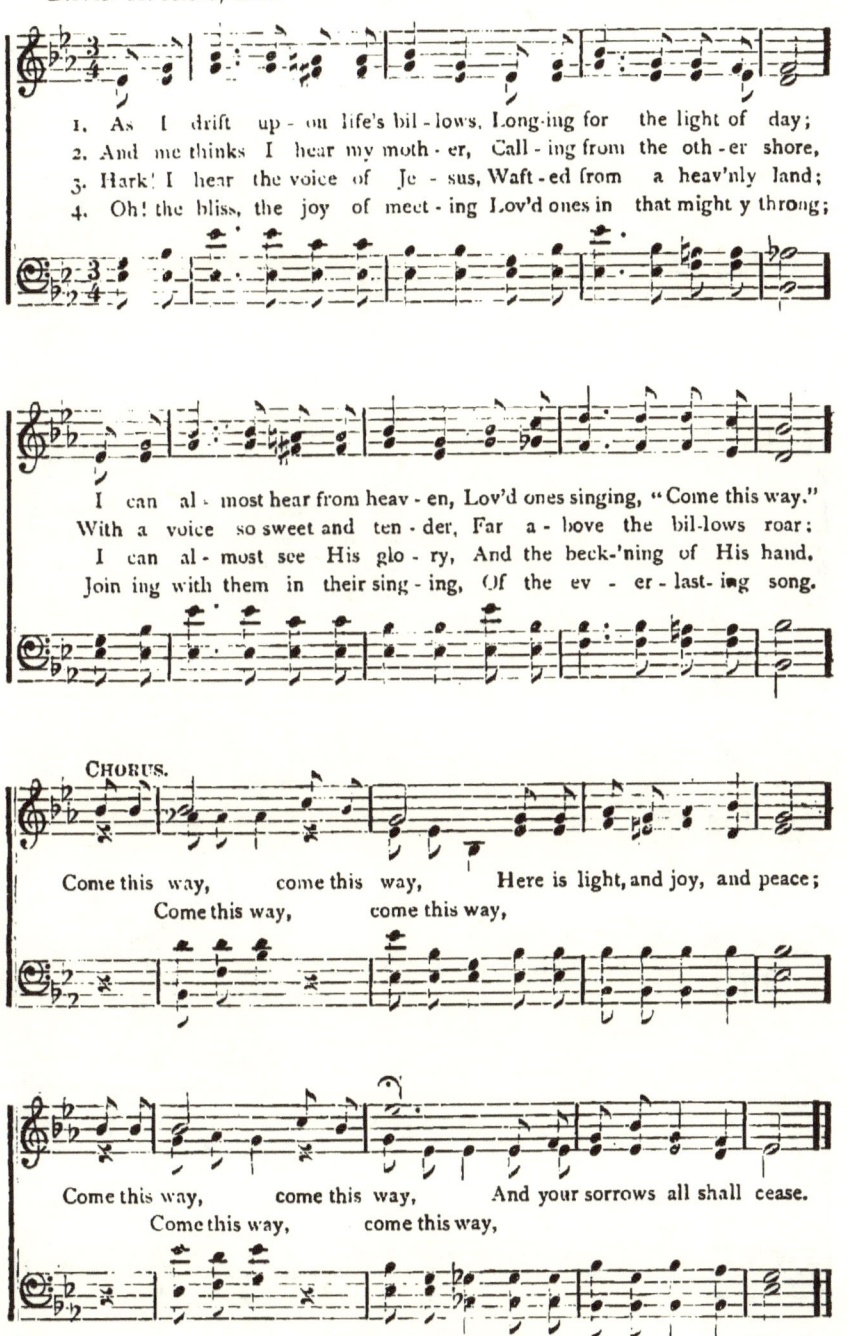

EVERY HOUR FOR JESUS.—Concluded.

Sav-iour, bless-ed Sav-iour, may this life be mine.

WALKING AS THE SPIRIT LEADS.

E. E. HEWITT. WM. J. KIRKPATRICK.

1. Let my steps be light and free, Walk-ing as the Spir-it leads,
2. In His Word, a guid-ing light; Walk-ing as the Spir-it leads,
3. Teach-ing me the Fa-ther's will, Walk-ing as the Spir-it leads,
4. Now am I God's hap-py child, Walk-ing as the Spir-it leads.

Bless-ed joy and lib-er-ty, Walk-ing as the Spir-it leads.
Star-ry beams for ev-'ry night, Walk-ing as the Spir-it leads.
Help-ing me to do it still Walk-ing as the Spir-it leads.
Par-doned, cleansed and rec-on-ciled Walk-ing as the Spir-it leads.

CHORUS.

Day by day, come what may, Grace a-bound-ing, for my needs
Strength to stay, all the way, Walk-ing as the Spir-it leads.

Copyright, 1897, by Wm. J. Kirkpatrick.

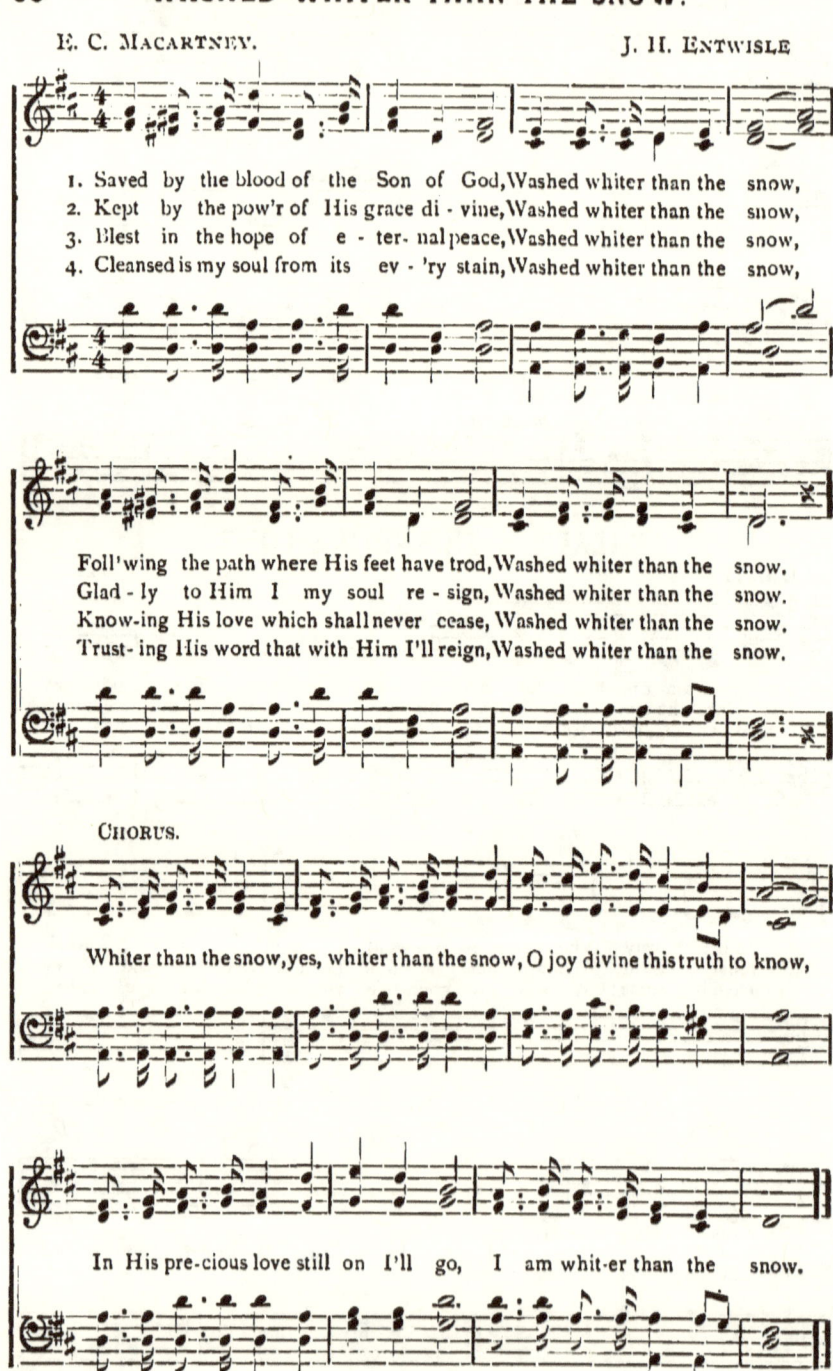

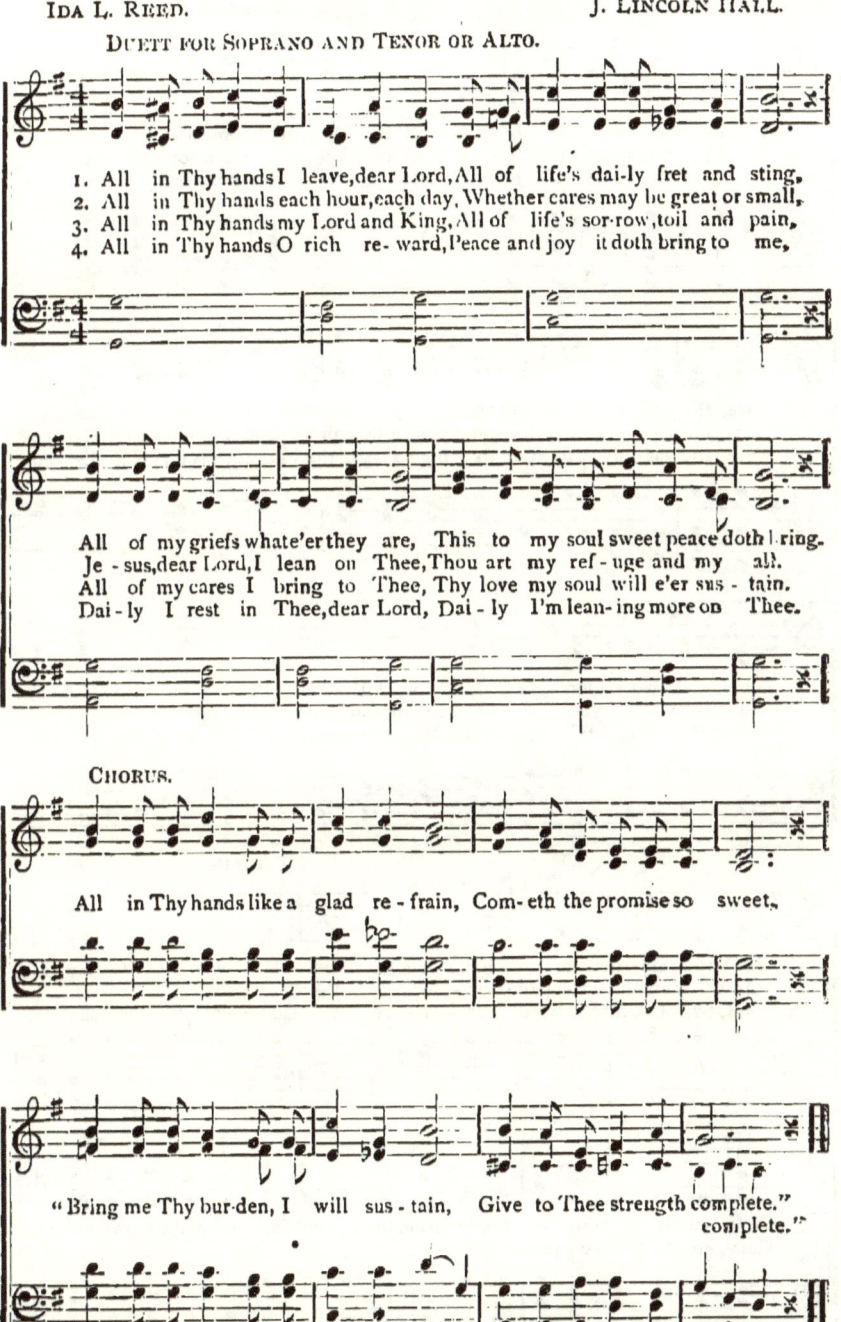

52. LIST TO THE VOICE OF JESUS.

Irvin H. Mack. Charles A. Bechter.

1. List the voice of Je-sus call-ing, Who will come and work to-day?
2. List the voice of Je-sus call-ing, There is work for ma-ny more;
3. List the voice of Je-sus call-ing, Is there noth-ing you can do?

See, the fields are white and read-y; Come and bear the sheaves away. Come, O
If you can-not cross the o-cean, You can work be-fore your door. Give the
See the ma-ny that are dy-ing; Haste! the Master calls for you. Do not

come, and work for Je-sus; Who will lend a help-ing hand? Gent-ly
Sav-iour all your tal-ents, Small and hum-ble though they be, He will
waste the use-ful mo-ments, Ma-ny sheaves are left for thee; Do your

CHORUS.

lead the sin-ner, to a hap-py land.
bless them with a crown of vic-to-ry.
best, 'twill live thro' all e-ter-ni-ty.

O come the Sav-iour calls,
Come while the day shall last,

Wait not till ev-'ning falls; Gather from the ripen'd fields What the harvest yields.
Come ere the harvest's past; (*Omit*........ •. ......)

Copyright, 1907, by Hall-Mack Co.

THERE IS CLEANSING. Concluded.

trust-ing child, And they shall be whit-er than the snow, whit-er than snow.
scar-let be, Yet they shall be whit-er than the snow, whit-er than snow.
crim-son be, Yet they shall be whit-er than the snow, whit-er than snow.

I HAVE A WONDERFUL SAVIOUR.

IRVIN H. MACK.   J. LINCOLN HALL.

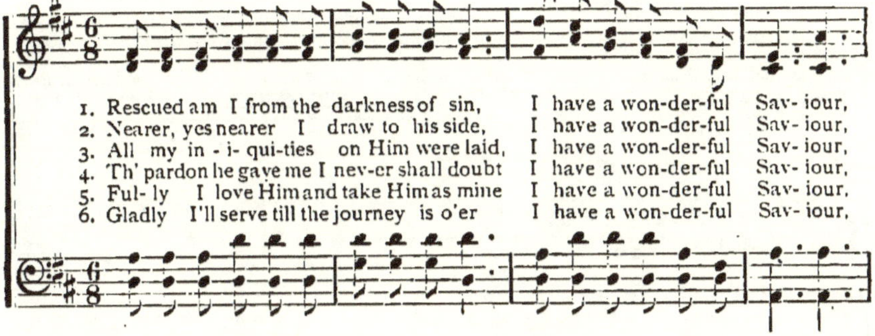

1. Rescued am I from the darkness of sin, I have a won-der-ful Sav-iour,
2. Nearer, yes nearer I draw to his side, I have a won-der-ful Sav-iour,
3. All my in-i-qui-ties on Him were laid, I have a won-der-ful Sav-iour,
4. Th' pardon he gave me I nev-er shall doubt I have a won-der-ful Sav-iour,
5. Ful-ly I love Him and take Him as mine I have a won-der-ful Sav-iour,
6. Gladly I'll serve till the journey is o'er I have a won-der-ful Sav-iour,

FINE.

Opened is Heav'n, I may now en-ter in, I have a won-der-ful Sav-iour.
Noth-ing can harm me no e-vil be-tide, I have a won-der-ful Sav-iour.
Cleansed and redeemed were the words that he said, I have a won-der-ful Sav-iour.
Sins of my life-time were all blotted out, I have a won-der-ful Sav-iour.
Glad-ly for him all of earth I re-sign, I have a won-der-ful Sav-iour.
Then with the ransom'd I'll dwell ev-er-more, I have a won-der-ful Sav-iour.

D. S.—He cleansed from sin, and spoke peace to my soul, I have a wonder-ful Sav-iour.

CHORUS.   D.S.

Won-der-ful, won-der-ful, Sav-iour, I have a wonder-ful Sav-iour,

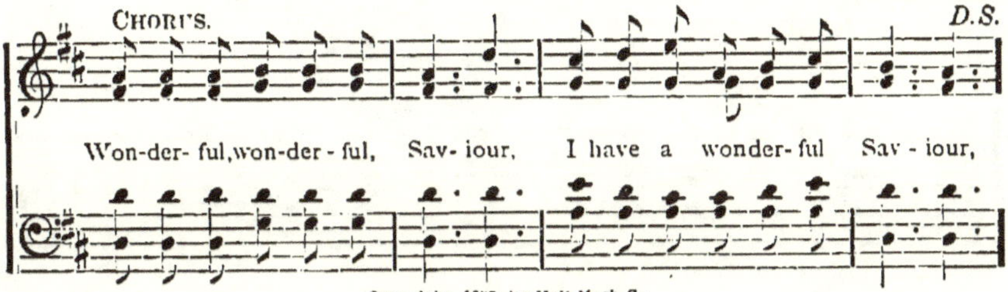

Copyright, 1897, by Hall-Mack Co.

Walking by the Saviour's Side.—Concluded.

walk - ing, Walk-ing where no harm can e'er be - tide.
walk-ing with Je - sus,

THERE IS A BRIGHT AND HAPPY HOME.

Adapted.   J. LINCOLN HALL.

1. There is a bright and hap-py home, Where all is joy and glad-ness,
2. This life is oft - en cloud-ed o'er, With tear - ful hours of sor - row,
3. There, all our fears are laid to rest, And hush'd in all our weep-ing,
4. We hope to reach this hap-py home, Where there is no more weep-ing,

Where sin and sor - row may not come, Nor an - y thought of sad - ness.
And those we hold so dear to - day, May go from us to - mor - row.
There, troub-led hearts find sweet re-pose, Like lit - tle chil-dren sleep - ing.
But wait in pa - tience God's own time, We still are in His keep - ing.

D.S.—Where we shall dwell in God's own light, For ev - er and for - ev - er.

D.S.

We love to think of that sweet home, Where death can part us nev - er,

Copyright, 1896, by Hall-Mack Co.

68   O BLESSED HOPE.
SOLO, DUET OR QUARTET.

E. E. Hewitt.   Wm. J. Kirkpatrick.

1. O bless- ed hope so dear, so bright, It cheers the watches of the night;
2. When dawns that hour of wondrous grace, No veil will hide my Saviour's face;
3. Sin, pain and death, on that sweet day, Like broken dreams, shall pass away;
4. Soon, soon shall fade the scenes of time, Emmanuel's advent bells shall chime;

It wakes a song with- in the soul, Till heav'nly hal - le - lu - jahs roll.
He'll own me ev - er- more as his, And I shall see him as he is.
His spot- less beau-ty I shall wear, His per- fect joy and glo - ry share.
The Bride shall hear the Bridegroom's voice; Look up, my heart, in him rejoice!

CHORUS. 1 John iii. 2.

Be - lov - ed, be- lov- ed, Now are we the sons of God, And it doth not

yet appear what we shall be; But we know that when he shall appear,
                                                  we know

We know that when he shall appear, We shall be like him, We shall be
        we know

1896, Copyright of Wm. J. Kirkpatrick. Used by permission.

O BLESSED HOPE.—Concluded.

poco ritard.

like him; For we shall see him as he is, We shall see him as he is:

a tempo.

We know that when he shall appear, We know that when he shall appear,
we know   we know

We shall be like him, We shall be like him; For we shall see him as he is.

MUST JESUS BEAR THE CROSS.
(MAITLAND. C. M.)

Thomas Shepherd. Alt.   G. N. Allen.

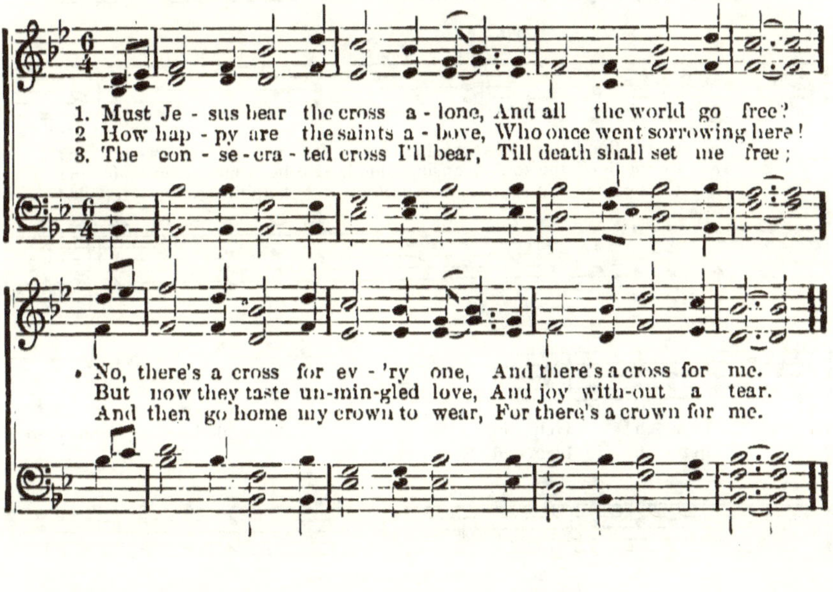

1. Must Je-sus bear the cross a-lone, And all the world go free?
2. How hap-py are the saints a-bove, Who once went sorrowing here!
3. The con-se-cra-ted cross I'll bear, Till death shall set me free;

No, there's a cross for ev-'ry one, And there's a cross for me.
But now they taste un-min-gled love, And joy with-out a tear.
And then go home my crown to wear, For there's a crown for me.

CLEANSING FOUNTAIN.—Concluded.

Where I may wash, may wash and be clean, O help me to enter in!

THE BEAUTIFUL SUNSHINE.

F. M. D.
FRANK M. DAVIS, by per.

1. Je-sus, the beau-ti-ful sun-shine, Changing the night in-to day,
2. Je-sus, the beau-ti-ful sun-shine, Shin-ing from por-tals a-bove,
3. Je-sus, the beau-ti-ful sun-shine, Shine in our lives ev-er-more,

Shed in our hearts Thy bright ra-diance, Sweet-ly il-lu-mine our way.
When all a-round us is dark-ness, Send us a gleam of Thy love.
May we re-flect Thy ef-ful-geance, As we have nev-er be-fore.

CHORUS.

Sun-shine, sun-shine, Je-sus, the beau-ti-ful sun-shine;

Sun-shine, sun-shine, Sweet-ly il-lu-mine our way.

Copyright, 1896, by Frank M. Davis.

GOOD NIGHT.—Concluded.

night till we meet at the Sav-iour's feet, In that land where all is bright.

WE'LL WORK TILL JESUS COMES.

Dr. MILLER.

1. O land of rest, for thee I sigh, When will the mo-ment come,
2. No tran-quil joys on earth I know, No peace ful, shelt'ring dome,
3. To Je-sus Christ I fled for rest; He bade me cease to roam.

When I shall lay my ar-mor by, And dwell in peace at home?
This world's a wil-der-ness of woe, This world is not my home.
And lean for suc-cor on His breast, And He'd con-duct me home.

CHORUS.

We'll work till Je-sus comes, We'll work till Je-sus comes,
Well w'ork   We'll work

We'll work till Je-sus comes, And we'll be gath-er'd home.
We'll work

THE CALL TO ZION.

GRACE ELIZABETH COBB.   CHAS. H. GABRIEL.

1. O watchman pac-ing Zi-on's hills, what ti-dings from a-far?
2. Lo, yon-der heav-en's por-tal opes— e-ter-ni-ty's in view,
3. O cit-y, set up-on a hill, hide not thine orb of light!

Lo, thro' the shad-ows dark and chill, breaks forth the Morn-ing Star!
Old things are van-ish-ing a-way, and all be-com-ing new!
Shine forth un-til it pierce the bounds of earth's re-mot-est night;

The dawn of im-mor-tal-i-ty is ope-ning on mine eye;
The King of kings sub-du-eth all His foes be-neath His feet,
'Till na-tions, yet a-far be drawn to own Mes-si-ah King.

Wake, Zi-on, wake from out thy sleep, thy Lord, thy Lord is nigh!
And summons thee, His blood-bought Bride, to share His roy-al seat.
And thou, with joy, un-to thy Lord the whole cre-a-tion bring.

Copyright, 1897, by Hall-Mack Co.

DREAMING OF HOME.

BIRDIE BELL.   J. HOWARD ENTWISLE.

1. When my heart is aching, wea- ry, And when all of life seems drear- y,
2. There the joy bells ne'er cease ringing, There the an- gel-choirs are sing- ing,
3. Home be- lov- ed, o'er death's river, Of which God Himself is Giv- er,

To the Home a- cross the riv - er   then my fan - cy wings its flight;
Ev- 'ry voice attuned to mu - sic   as they join the heav'nly hymn;
How I love to read the sto - ry   of thy peer- less beauties o'er;

There is nev - er sound of weeping, And no anx- ious vig - il keeping,
'Tis the same old blessed sto - ry, "Glo- ry in the high- est, glo - ry,
New the tale, although so old - en, Of the pavements rich and gold- en,

Nev - er o'er its walls of jas- per falls the shade of sorrow's night.
Crown the Sav - iour with a di - a - dem that time can nev - er dim."
Of the Cit - y bathed in ra - di- ance, just on the oth - er shore.

Copyright 1887, by Hall Mack Co.

DREAMING OF HOME.—Concluded. 79

4 Nevermore shall I be sighing,
 And there will be no more dying,
Heaven's gate is but the entrance to a never-ending life;
 There is joy for all our sorrow,
 In the blest and longed for morrow,
There my heart will rest in quiet after this world's empty strife.

5 O my soul, be patient ever,
 And be earnest thine endeavor,
To do work for Christ thy Master as the moments speed away;
 In His own time He will call thee
 Where no ill can e'er befall thee,
To the City of the faithful just beyond the gates of day.

THE GRACIOUS CALL.—Concluded. 83

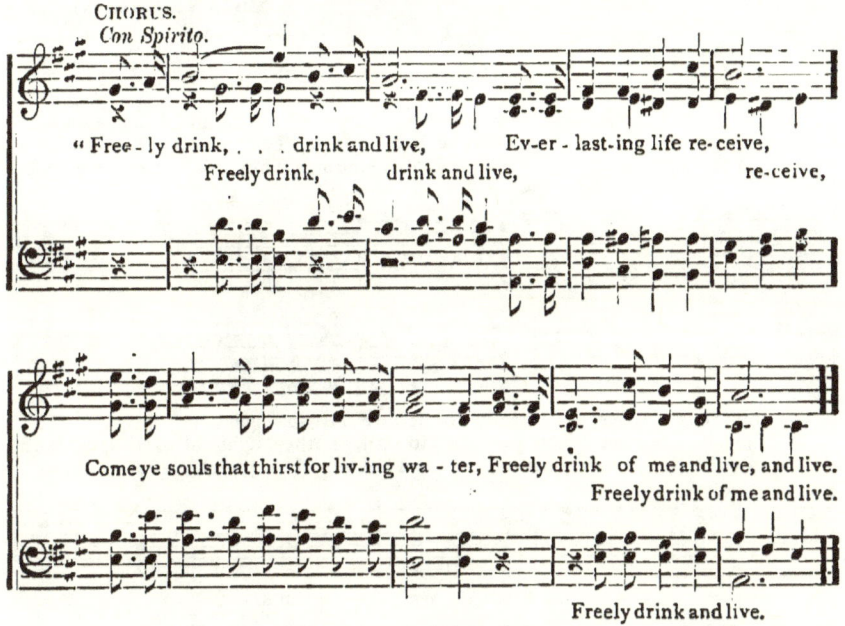

JESUS! NAME OF WONDROUS LOVE.

L. M. GOTTSCHALK.

84. PRAISE HIM FOREVER.

C. W.   CHAS. H. GABRIEL.

1. O what shall I do my Saviour to praise, So faithful and true, so plent'ous in grace, So strong to deliver, so good to redeem, The weakest believer that hangs upon Him.
2. How happy the man whose heart is set free, The people that can be joyful in Thee! Their joy is to walk in the light of His face, And talk of His infinite wonderful grace.
3. Yes, Lord, I shall see the bliss of Thine own, Thy secret to me shall soon be made known; For sorrow and sadness I joy shall receive, And share in the gladness of all that believe.

CHORUS.

I'll give Him my worship, my service, my all, His name I will laud, and His goodness extol; Praise Him forever, exultingly sing, Jesus, my Saviour, Redeemer, and King.

Copyright, 1897, by Hall-Mack Co.

REDEMPTION. 87

Isaiah Toy.
J. Lincoln Hall.

1. A sinner though I am, Of darkest, deepest shade, A righteousness I claim, My own thro' Jesus made. Unnumber'd worlds could not atone, But Jesus bore my sins alone, But
2. This love ineffable My heart hath prepossessed, And filled my fervid soul With wonder unexpress'd; For tho't or word seeks but in vain The holy mys-t'ry to explain, The
3. 'Well might seraphic tongues Be mute, with sacred awe; And heav'n's sublimest songs Suspend, while angels saw A glimpse of what could not be told, Nor can eternity unfold, Nor
4. Heav'n's unexampled love To man, in Christ displayed, Shall endless wonder prove, Unfathomed, unportrayed. Eternal love! The Offended dies To bring the offender to the skies, To

CHORUS.

Saved, Saved;
Jesus bore my sins alone,
holy mys-t'ry to explain,
can eternity unfold,
bring the offender to the skies.
Saved, O yes, I'm saved, Saved, O yes, I'm saved;

Saved,
Thro' Jesus' blood and righteousness, I now am saved: Saved, O yes, I'm saved,

Copyright, 1896, by Hall-Mack Co.

REDEMPTION.—Concluded.

Saved; O yes, I'm saved; Thro' Jesus' blood and righteousness, I now am saved.

KEEP ME NEAR THE BLESSED SAVIOUR.

E. C. MACARTNEY.   J. LINCOLN HALL.

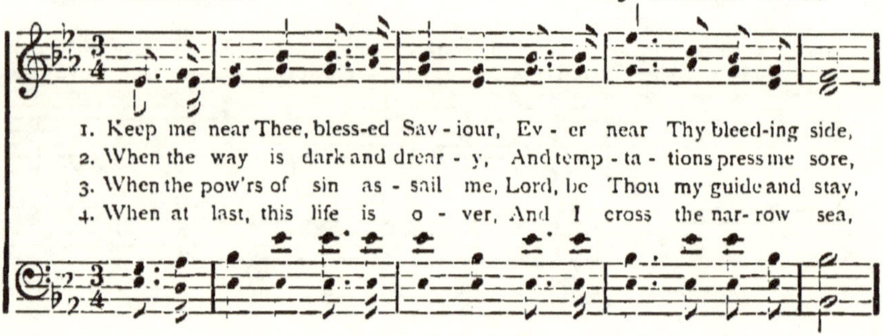

1. Keep me near Thee, bless-ed Sav-iour, Ev - er near Thy bleed-ing side,
2. When the way is dark and drear - y, And temp - ta - tions press me sore,
3. When the pow'rs of sin as - sail me, Lord, be Thou my guide and stay,
4. When at last, this life is o - ver, And I cross the nar - row sea,

Though my faint - ing heart may wav - er, Let me in Thy love a - bide.
When my halt - ing steps grow wea - ry, Draw me to Thee, more and more.
By Thy gra - cious pow - er lead me, Un - to ev - er - last - ing day.
Let Thy spir - it o'er me hov - er, Take my ransomed soul to Thee.

D.S.—Show to me Thy gra - cious fa - vor, Cheer my way with heavenly light.

CHORUS.   D.S.

Keep me near Thee, bless-ed Sav - iour, Guide my trembling steps a - right,

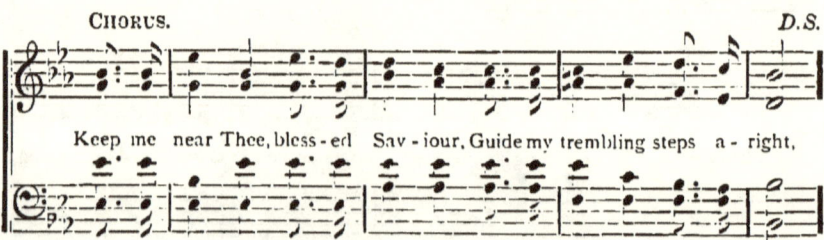

Copyright, 1897, by Hall-Mack Co.

90. A BLESSING IN PRAYER.

E. E. HEWITT.   WM. J. KIRKPATRICK.

1. There is rest, sweet rest, at the Master's feet, There is fa-vor now at the mer-cy seat, For a-ton-ing blood has been sprinkled there; There is
2. There is grace to help in our time of need, For our Friend above is a Friend in-deed, We may cast on him ev-'ry grief and care; There is
3. When our songs are glad with the joy of life, When our hearts are sad with its ills and strife, When the powers of sin would the soul ensnare, There is
4. There is per-fect peace tho' the wild waves roll; There are gifts of love for the seek-ing soul, Till we praise the Lord in his home so fair; There is

CHORUS.

al-ways a blessing, a blessing in pray'r. There's a blessing in pray'r, in be-lieving pray'r; When our Saviour's name to the throne we bear, Then a Father's love will re-ceive us there; There is al-ways a blessing, a blessing in pray'r.

1887, Copyright of Wm. J. Kirkpatrick. Used by permission.

PERISHING SOULS.—Concluded. 93

I SURRENDER ALL.

J. W. Van DeVenter. W. S. Weeden.
DUET.

1. All to Jesus I surrender, All to Him I freely give;
   I will ever love and trust Him, In His presence daily live.
2. All to Jesus I surrender, Humbly at His feet I bow,
   Worldly pleasures all forsaken, Take me, Jesus, take me now.
3. All to Jesus I surrender, Make me, Saviour wholly Thine;
   Let me feel the Holy Spirit, Truly know that Thou art mine.

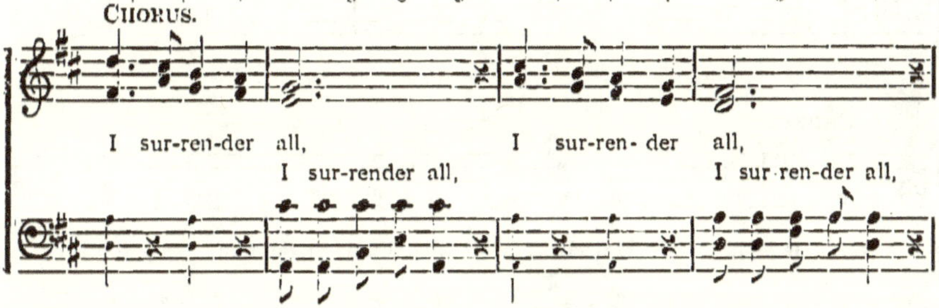

CHORUS.

I surrender all, I surrender all,
I surrender all, I surrender all,
All to Thee, my blessed Saviour, I surrender all.

4 All to Jesus I surrender,
  Lord, I give myself to Thee,
  Fill me with Thy love and power,
  Let Thy blessing fall on me.

5 All to Jesus I surrender,
  Now I feel the sacred flame;
  O the joy of full salvation!
  Glory, glory to His name!

Copyright, 1896, by Weeden & Van DeVenter.

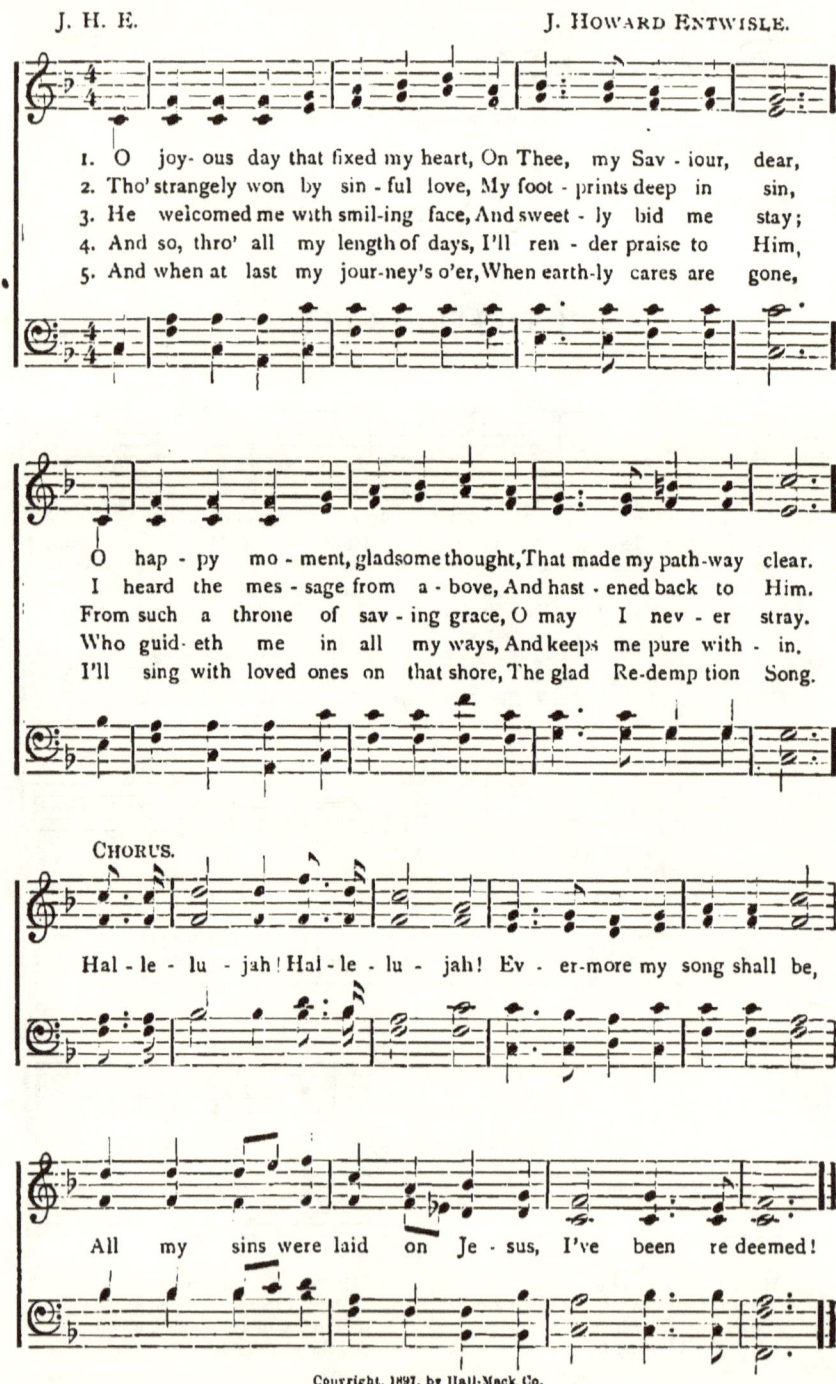

96. TILL MY FATHER BIDS ME COME.

IDA L. REED.   J. HOWARD ENTWISLE.

1. Till my Father bids me come To the rest a-waiting me, To my bless-ed, happy home Let me tar-ry pa-tient-ly; Fret-ting not, tho' days are long, Working for His king-dom fair, Sing-ing hope's sweet, happy song, Till He calls me o-ver there.

2. Till my Father bids me come Let me fill the passing days, Each with ten-der deeds of love, Songs of joy, of trust and praise, By His bless-ed aid di-vine, Let me spread a-broad love's light, Till the world a-bout me shine With it's ra-di-ance so bright.

3. Till my Father bids me come Let me wait His ho-ly will, Toil-ing for Him ev-er-more, Watching for His com-ing still. When He bids me come at last, Hap-py, hap-py I shall be, All my wait-ing, toil-ing, past When my bless-ed home I see.

CHORUS.

Till my Father bids me come, Let me ev-er patient be, Doing all I can for Him, Till my happy home I see.

Copyright, 1897, by Hall-Mack Co.

HE IS MY SAVIOUR DIVINE.

IRVIN H. MACK.   J. LINCOLN HALL.

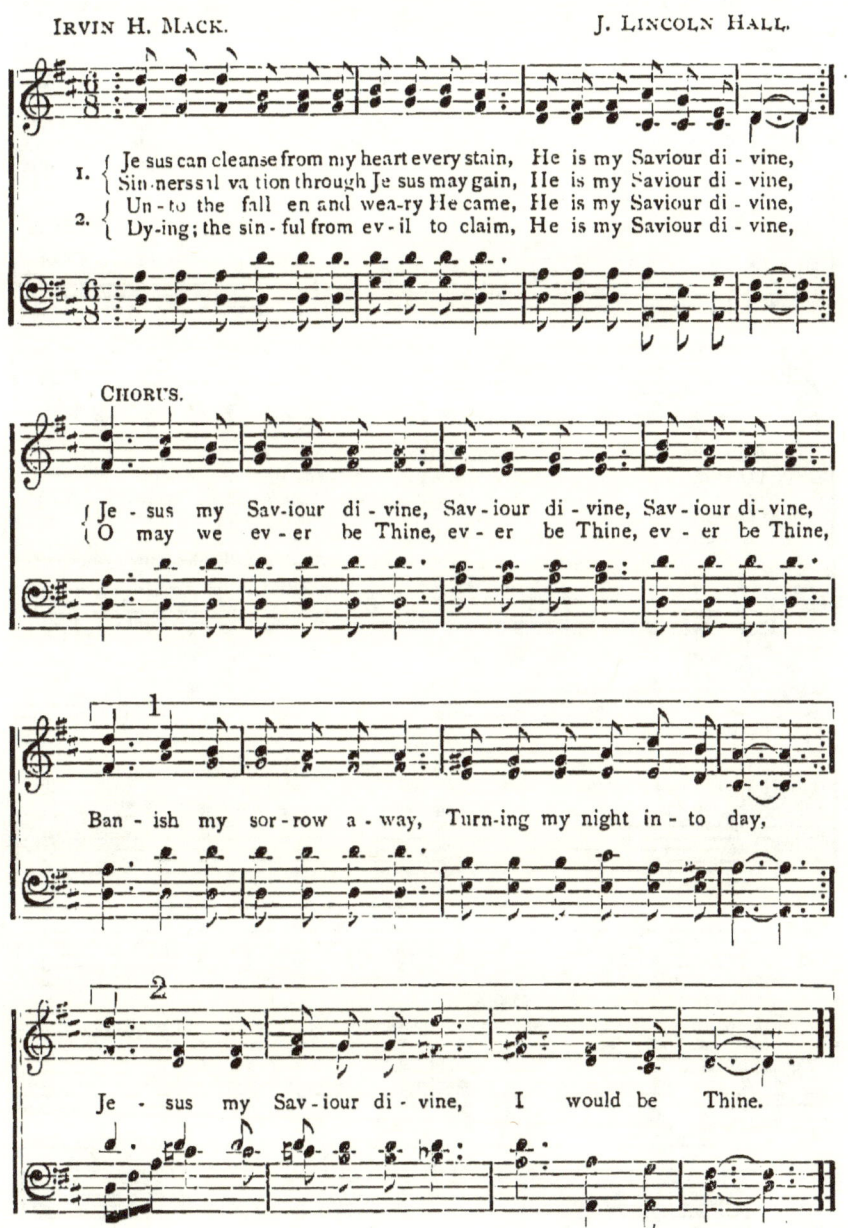

1. { Jesus can cleanse from my heart every stain, He is my Saviour divine,
   { Sinners salvation through Jesus may gain, He is my Saviour divine,
2. { Unto the fallen and weary He came, He is my Saviour divine,
   { Dying; the sinful from evil to claim, He is my Saviour divine,

CHORUS.
{ Jesus my Saviour divine, Saviour divine, Saviour divine,
{ O may we ever be Thine, ever be Thine, ever be Thine,
Banish my sorrow away, Turning my night into day,
Jesus my Saviour divine, I would be Thine.

3 Sunshine for shadow He ever will give,
  He is my Saviour divine,
Blessings for all who His promise receive,
  He is my Saviour divine.

4 Water for them that are thirsting is free,
  He is my Saviour divine,
With the redeemed through His blood we
  He is my Saviour divine. [may be,

Copyright, 1897, by Hall-Mack Co.

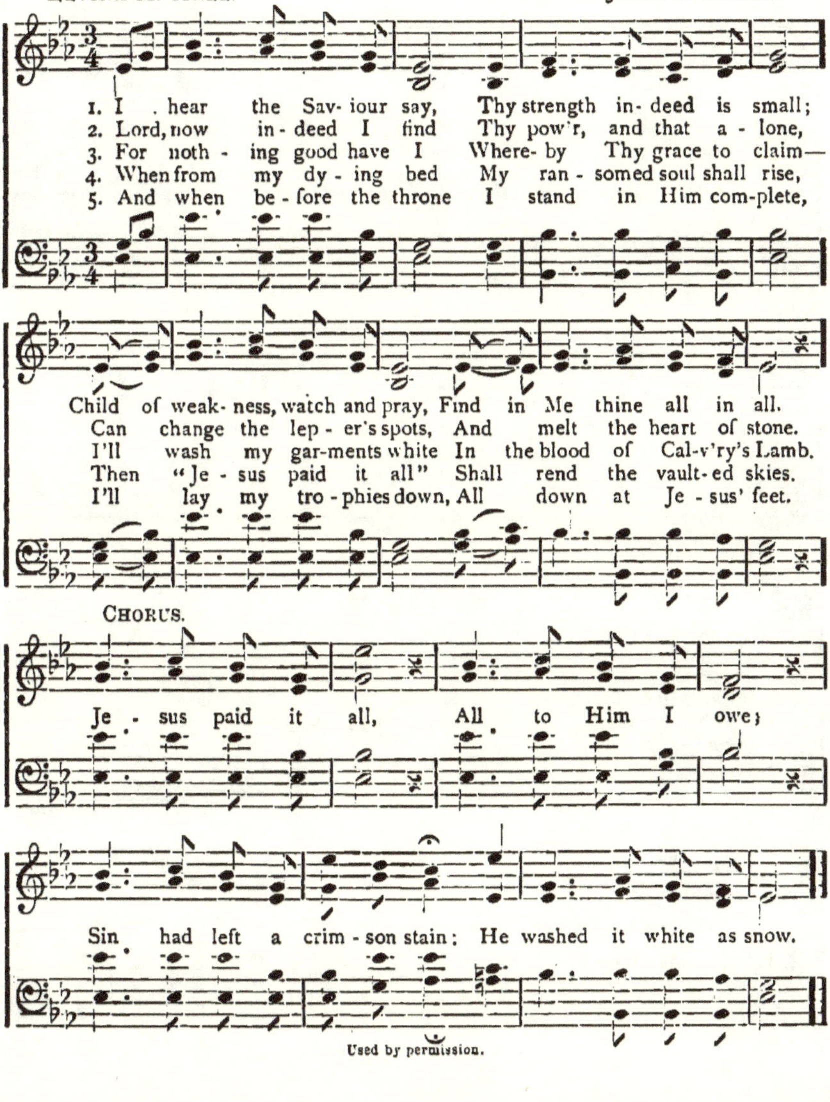

AND SHALL I TURN BACK? 105

Arr. by GRACE WEISER DAVIS.

1. My Jesus, I love Thee, I know Thou art mine, For Thee all the follies of sin I resign; My gracious Redeemer, my Saviour art Thou; If ever I loved Thee, my Jesus, 'tis now.
2. I love Thee because Thou hast first loved me, And purchased my pardon on Calvary's tree; I love Thee for wearing the thorns on Thy brow; If ever I loved Thee, my Jesus, 'tis now.
3. I'll love Thee in life, I will love Thee in death, And praise Thee as long as Thou givest me breath, And say when the death-dew lies cold on my brow; If ever I loved Thee, my Jesus, 'tis now.
4. In mansions of glory and endless delight, I'll ever adore Thee in heaven so bright; I'll sing with the glittering crown on my brow; If ever I loved Thee, my Jesus, 'tis now.

CHORUS.

And shall I turn back in-to the world? O, no, not I, not I!
I'll never turn back, never turn back, O, no, not I, not I!
And shall I turn back in-to the world? No, no, not I!
I'll never turn back, never turn back, O, no, not I!

Copyright, 1894, by Grace Weiser Davis. Used by per.

114. TRUSTING IN THE PROMISES.

F. M. D. F. M. D., by per.

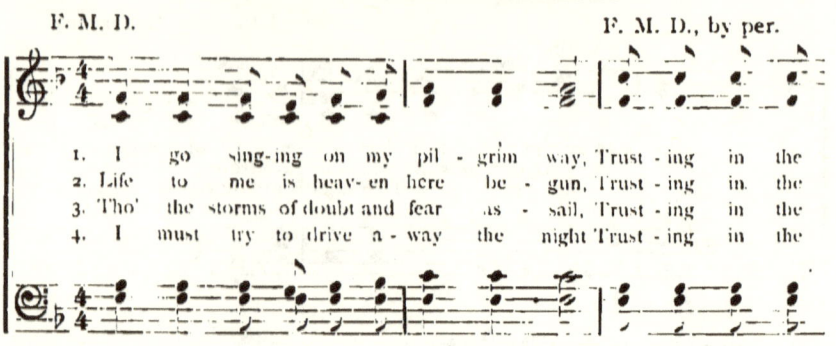

1. I go sing-ing on my pil-grim way, Trust-ing in the
2. Life to me is heav-en here be-gun, Trust-ing in the
3. Tho' the storms of doubt and fear as-sail, Trust-ing in the
4. I must try to drive a-way the night Trust-ing in the

prom-is-es of Je-sus; Now my soul is hap-py ev-'ry day,
prom-is-es of Je-sus; I will la-bor till my race is run,
prom-is-es of Je-sus; They can nev-er ov-er me pre-vail,
prom-is-es of Je-sus; Lead some soul in-to the gos-pel light,

CHORUS.

Trusting in the prom-is-es of Je-sus.
Trusting in the prom-is-es of Je-sus.
Trusting in the prom-is-es of Je-sus.
Trusting in the prom-is-es of Je-sus. } Joy is mine, peace di-vine,

A SHOUT OF VICTORY. Concluded.

free,............... 'Tis a shout...... ...... of vic - to - ry...vic-to - ry.
of grace so free, 'Tis a shout, the shout of vic - to - ry.

THAT BLESSED HOPE.

G. A. WARBURTON.   W. S. WEEDEN.

1. Im - pa - tient heart, be still, be still! What tho' He tar - ries long? What
2. My ea - ger heart, be still, be still! Thy Lord will sure - ly come, And
3. My an - xious heart, be still, be still! Watch, pray, and work, and then It

tho' the tri - umph song Is still de - layed? Thou hast His pro - mise sure,
take thee to His home, With Him to dwell. It may not be to - day,
will not mat - ter when Thy Lord shall come. At mid-night or at noon,

And that is all se - cure, Be not a - fraid, be not a - fraid!
And yet, my soul, it may; I can - not tell, I can - not tell!
He can - not come too soon To take thee home, to take thee home!

Copyright, 1896, by W. S. Weeden.

COME TO THE MIGHTY TO SAVE.

HARRIET E. JONES.   J. HOWARD ENTWISLE.

1. Are you in by-ways of sor-row and sin? Come to the Might-y to save!.... Would you the life of the chris-tian be-gin? Come to the Might-y to save! Lo! He is call-ing in ten-der-est tone, Wait-ing this mo-ment to
2. Claim-ing the prom-ise and claiming it now, Come to the Might-y to save!.... None ev-er per-ished where pen-i-tents bow, Come to the Might-y to save! Kneel to our Sav-iour, con-fess and be-lieve, While you are ask-ing, free
3. Pre-cious the prom-ise contained in the word, Come to the Might-y to save!.... All may be saved who be-lieve on our Lord, Come to the Might-y to save! Come and be clothed in the gar-ment of white, Come, and be heir with the

Copyright, 1897, by Hall-Mack Co.

COME TO THE MIGHTY TO SAVE.—Concluded. 119

call you His own You may find mer - cy low
par - don re - ceive, Dare not, my broth - er, the
souls on the right, Come to our bless - ed Re -

down at His throne, Come to the Might - y to save!
Spir - it to grieve Come to the Might - y to save!
deem - er to - night, Who is so will - ing to save!

CHORUS.

Come to the Might - y to save! . . . . Come to the
 to save

Might - y to save! . . . . "Come!" He is call - ing in
 to save

ten - der - est tone, Oh! He is might - y to save. . . .
 to save

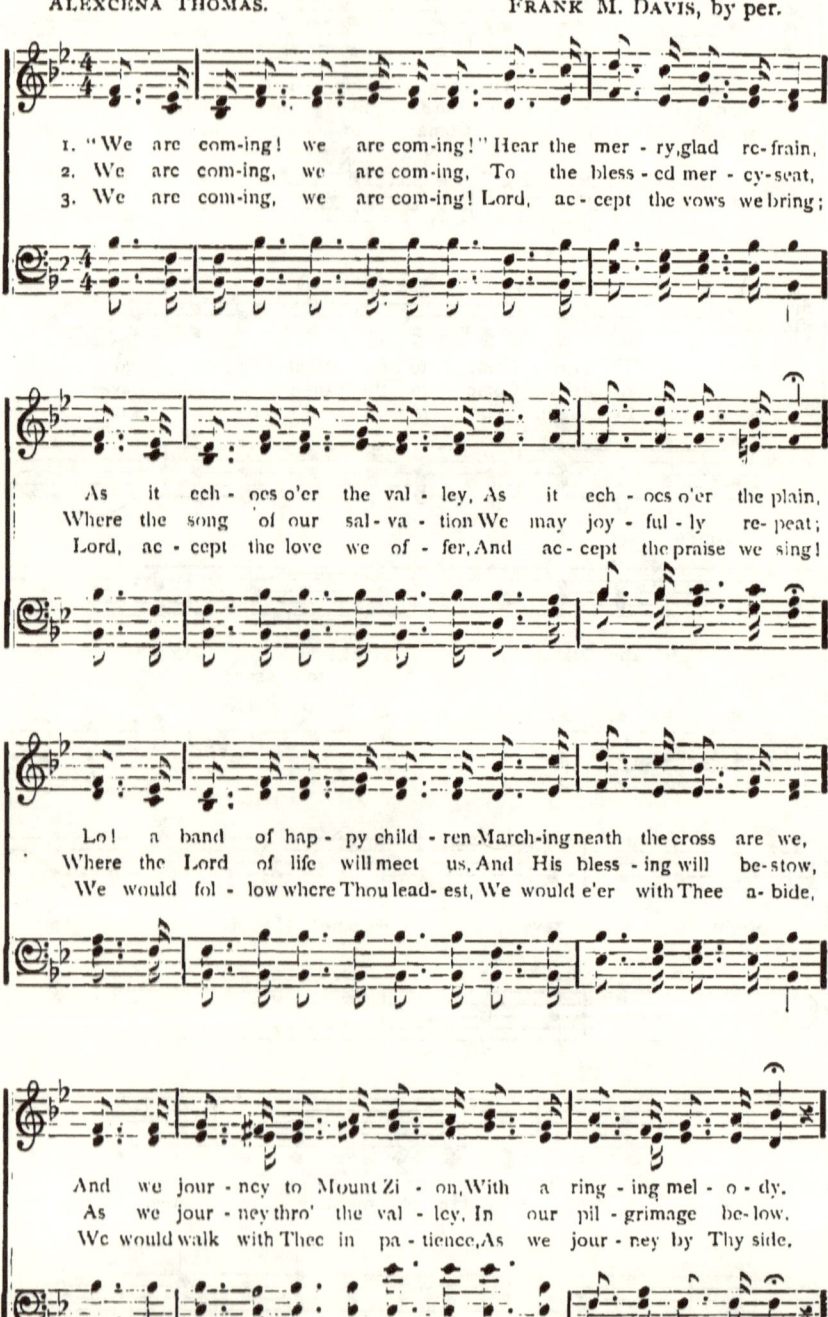

HE SAVES ME.—Concluded.

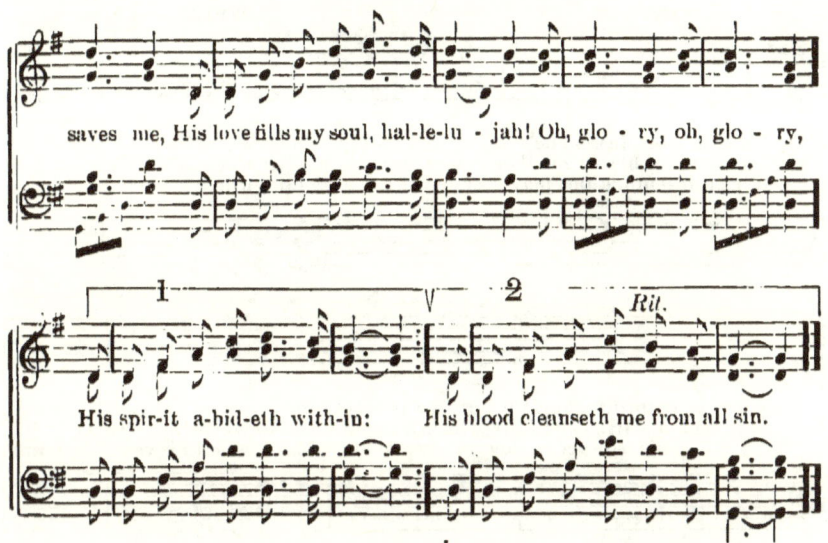

saves me, His love fills my soul, hal-le-lu - jah! Oh, glo - ry, oh, glo - ry,

His spir-it a-bid-eth with-in: His blood cleanseth me from all sin.

ALAS! AND DID MY SAVIOUR BLEED?
ISAAC WATTS.

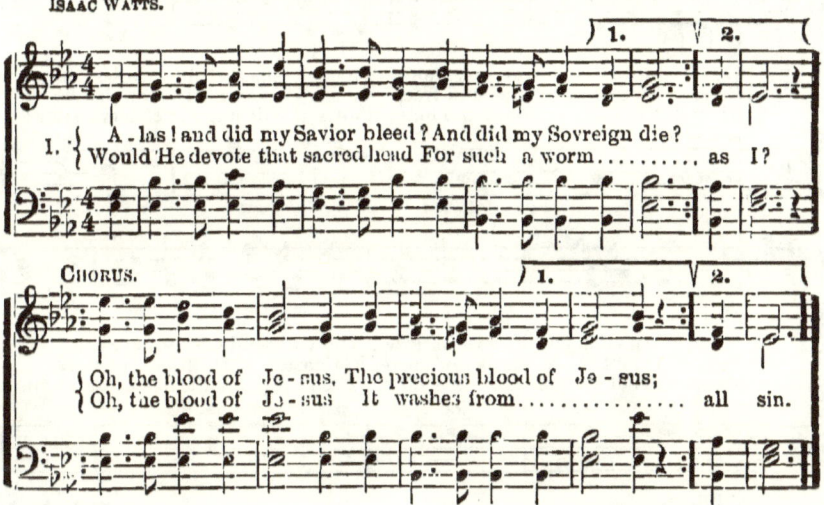

1. A - las! and did my Savior bleed? And did my Sovreign die?
Would He devote that sacred head For such a worm.......... as I?

CHORUS.

Oh, the blood of Je - sus, The precious blood of Je - sus;
Oh, the blood of Je - sus It washes from.......... all sin.

2 Was it for crimes that I have done,
  He groaned upon the tree?
  Amazing pity! grace unknown!
  And love beyond degree!

3 Well might the sun in darkness hide,
  And shut his glories in,
  When Christ, the mighty Maker, died,
  For man the creature's sin.

4 Thus might I hide my blushing face
  While His dear cross appears;
  Dissolve my heart in thankfulness,
  And melt mine eyes to tears.

5 But drops of grief can ne'er repay
  The debt of love I owe;
  Here, Lord, I give myself away,—
  'Tis all that I can do.

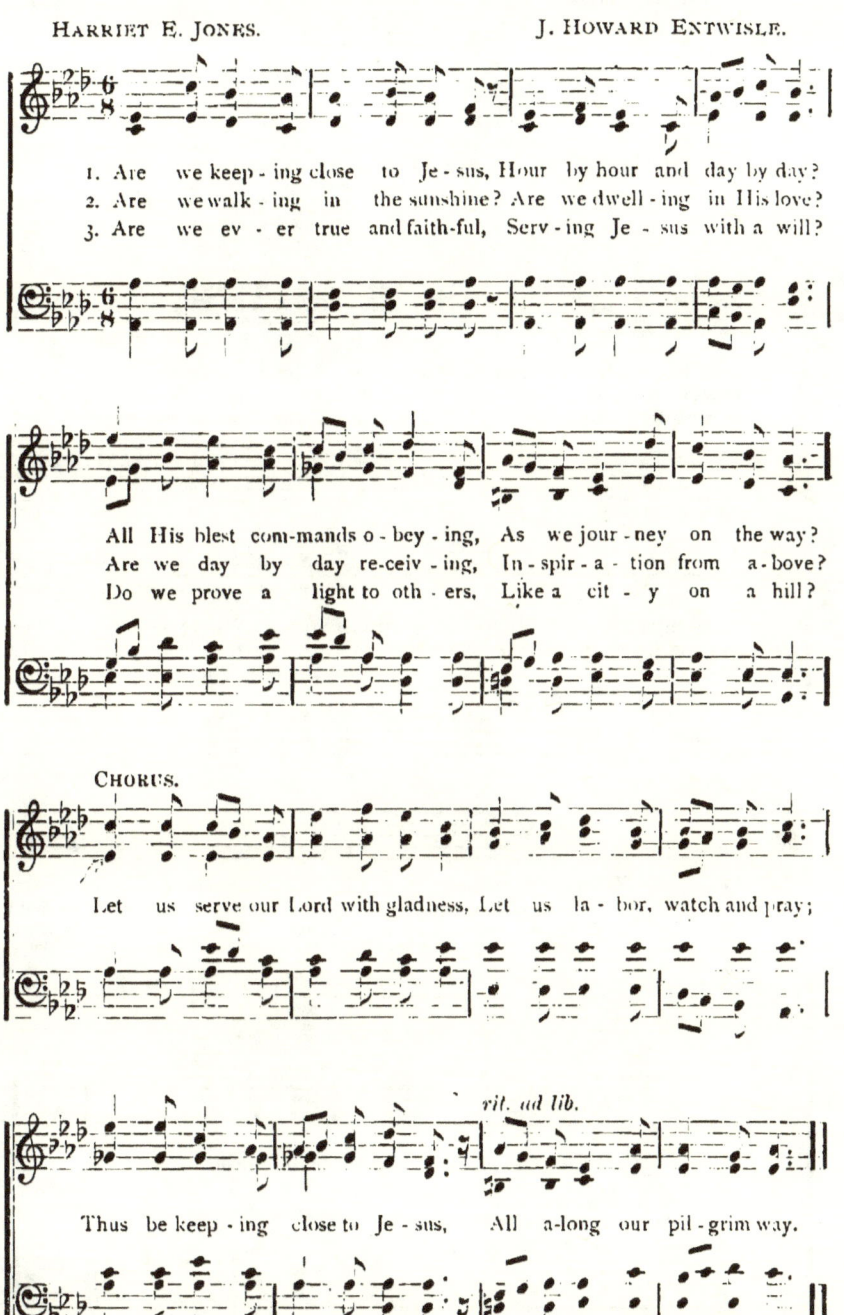

130 LOOK TO JESUS.

IDA L. REED. CHAS. A. BECHTER.

1. Look to Je - sus, He will save thee, Tho' the tem-pest ra - ges high;
2. Look to Je - sus, He will save thee, Tho' thou'rt tempted oft and tried,
3. Look to Je - sus, then for - ev - er, Look to Him in faith and love,

Trust in Him, His love un - fail - ing Will not let thee help-less die.
He thy soul from sin will res - cue, 'Twas for this Thy Sav - iour died.
Sing thy heart's sweet songs of glad-ness, He will bless thee from a - bove.

CHORUS.

Look to Je - sus He will save thee, Trust in Him from day to day,

He will keep thee, He will strengthen, Guard and guide thy steps al - way.

Copyright, 1897, by Hall-Mack Co.

THE BRIGHT MORNING-LAND.—Concluded. 137

by Thy hand,...... Lead us to the Morn-ing-Land.

HOME TO REST.

(Can be used as a Solo, Duet or Quartet with Chorus.)

Rev. JOHNSON OATMAN, Jr.   Wm. J. KIRKPATRICK.

1. When-e'er my work on earth is done I'll face the glow-ing west
2. I'll trust in Je-sus, come what may, He'll help me when op-pressed;
3. I know what ev-er lot I share, My Fa-ther's will is best,
4. Some day be-side the crys-tal sea I'll stand a-mong the blest,

And calm-ly view life's set-ting sun, And then go home to rest.
I'll fol-low Him till close of day, And then go home to rest.
So while I live my cross I'll bear, And then go home to rest.
For soon my Lord will call for me, Then I'll go home to rest.

CHORUS.

Home .... to rest,............ Home.............. to rest,.........
Home to rest, home to rest, Home to rest in my Saviour's breast,

My la-bor done, at the set of sun, I'm go-ing home to rest.

Copyright, 1897, by Wm. J. Kirkpatrick.

MY BUD IN HEAVEN.

F. I. Darling.
W. S. Weeden.

1. A bud the gard'ner gave me, A fair and love-ly child,
   He gave it for my keep-ing To cher-ish un-de-filed;
   It lay up-on my bo-som It was my joy and pride,
   Per-haps it was an i-dol Which I must be de-nied.

2. For just as it was ope-ning In glo-ry to the day,
   Down came the heavenly gard-'ner And took my bud a-way;
   Yet not in wrath He took it A smile was on His face
   And ten-der-ly and kind-ly He bore it from its place.

3. "Fear not" methought He whis-pered "Thy bud shall be re-stored,
   I take it but to plant it, In the gar-den of my Lord;"
   And bade me not to sor-row As those who hope-less weep,
   For He who gave hath tak-en And He who took can keep.

4. And night and morn to-geth-er By the o-pen gate of prayer,
   I'll go un-to my dar-ling And sit be-side him there;
   I know for me 'twill o-pen Poor sin-ner though I be,
   For He who guards and keeps it Will keep my bud for me.

Copyright, 1897, by W. S. Weeden.

140. WE WILL SET UP OUR BANNERS.

JENNIE WILSON. HOWARD E. SMITH.
Con spirito.

1. In the name of our God we will set up our ban - ners,
2. We will set up the ban - ners of love and sal - va - tion,
3. In the glo - ri - ous ar - my en - list - ed for Je - sus
4. Tho' the march-ing be long and the con - flict be wea - ry,

And pro-claim the glad ti - dings from mount - ain and plain,
In the name of our God, which en - dur - eth for aye,
We will seek to keep step with the faith - ful and strong,
With the vis - ion of faith our re - ward we now view,

Grand - ly on - ward the cause of our Lord is ad - vanc - ing,
More and more shall the pow'r of our Lord be ex - alt - ed
And led on by the Lord, in His strength o - ver-com - ing,
Lov - ing praise from our Mas - ter, palm- branch - es of glo - ry

Truth tri - umph-ant o'er er - ror for - ev - er shall reign.
Till the na - tions of earth all shall yield to His sway.
We will sing with re - joic - ing the con - quer - or's song.
And life's crown shall be ours when the war - fare is through.

CHORUS.

In the name of our God we will set up our ban - ners,

Copyright, 1897, by Hall-Mack Co.

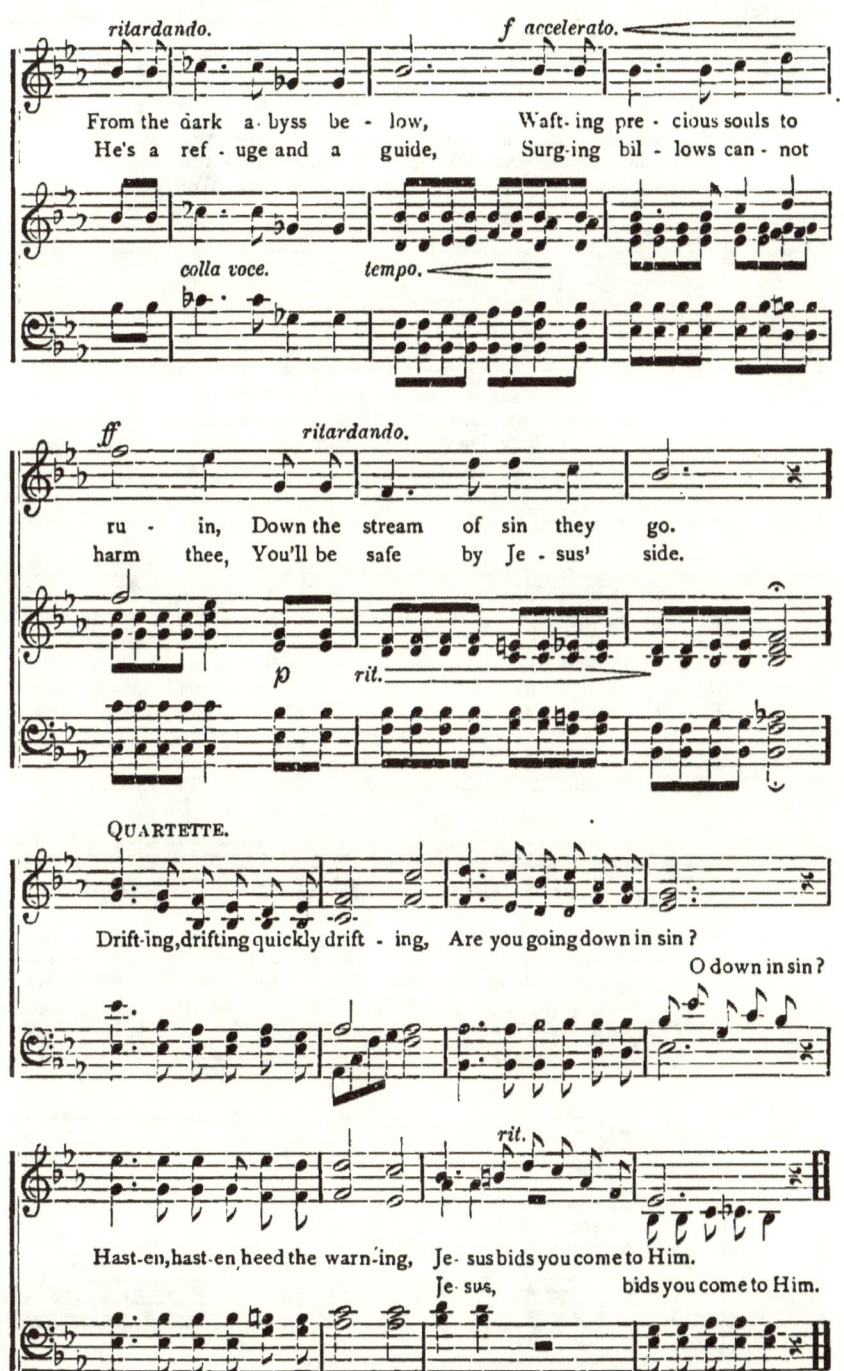

WORK FOR THE MASTER.—Concluded. 147

fill'd with His love, Work, work, work, work, Fill'd with His boundless love.

LORD, I'M COMING HOME.

W. J. K.   W. J. KIRKPATRICK.

With great feeling.

1. I've wan-dered far a-way from God, Now I'm com-ing home;
2. I've wast-ed ma-ny pre-cious years, Now I'm com-ing home;
3. I've tired of sin and stray-ing, Lord, Now I'm com-ing home;
4. My soul is sick, my heart is sore, Now I'm com-ing home;

The paths of sin too long I've trod, Lord, I'm com-ing home.
I now re-pent with bit-ter tears, Lord, I'm com-ing home.
I'll trust Thy love, be-lieve Thy word, Lord, I'm com-ing home.
My strength re-new, my hope re-store, Lord, I'm com-ing home.

D. S.—O-pen wide Thine arms of love, Lord, I'm com-ing home.

CHORUS.

Com-ing home, com-ing home, Nev-er more to roam;

5 My only hope, my only plea,
   Now I'm coming home,
That Jesus died, and died for me,
   Lord, I'm coming home.

6 I need His cleansing blood I know,
   Now I'm coming home;
O, wash me whiter than the snow,
   Lord, I'm coming home.

Copyright, 1892, by Wm. J. Kirkpatrick.

I HAVE FOUND A PRECIOUS SAVIOUR. Concluded. 149

true; I have found Him, I have
Saviour kind and true, so kind and true; I have found a precious friend, I have
found ... Him,
found a friend so true, O that you would find the precious Saviour too, the Saviour too.

WHEN THE WAY IS SO DARK.

EMILY P. MILLER.   J. LINCOLN HALL.

1. When the way is so dark That I scarce-ly can see, A dear lov-ing
2. His eye is on me In dark-ness or light, In storm or in
3. Then when death comes at last, And the Jor-dan I see; O Je-sus, my

Sav-iour Calls sweet-ly to me; He bids me look up-ward, Tho' the
sunshine, His love al-ways bright; In sleeping or wak-ing, Where-
Sav-iour, My Guide Thou shalt be; Tho' storm-y the wa-ters, Tho'

skies are so dim, He bids me press onward, Cling clos-er to Him.
ev-er I be, I know He is watching, And car-ing for me.
dark swells the tide, No fears shall a-larm me, When I'm at Thy side.

Copyright, 1895, by Hall-Mack Co.

PRESSING ONWARD. 153

R. H.   RICHARD HARDING.

1. "Forward to bat-tle!" hear now the call—Some, fainter-hearted, back-ward fall,
2. Stern is the con-flict, yet we shall win,—Tho' for our foes we've death and sin,
3. Soon 'twill be o'er, the vic-to-ry ours, Tho' now the front of bat-tle lowers,

Stay not to ques-tion,—here lies the way. We've naught to do but o - bey.
Close by our side stands Je - sus, our Lord. We may re - ly on His word.
Trust we our Lead-er,—He'll help us thro', He's ev - er strong and true.

REFRAIN.

On - ward! On - ward! ev - er press - ing on - ward—Bear - ing high our
stand-ard thro' the thick-est fight— On-ward! on-ward! ev - er press-ing on - ward,
Till in tri - umph we shall stand in heav'n's glo - ri - ous light.

Copyright, 1897, by Hall-Mack Co.

AT THE CALLING OF THE ROLL.—Concluded. 157

At the call - - - - ing of the roll
Call-ing of the roll, the call-ing of the roll,

Oh will you and I be there, In the won-'drous bliss to share,

When re-deemed ones an-swer, Present, At the call-ing of the roll?

HOSANNA, BE THE CHILDREN'S SONG.

Joyous.

1. Ho - san - na, be the chil-dren's song To Christ, the children's King;
2. Ho - san - na, on the wings of light O'er earth and o-cean fly;
3. Ho - san - na, then our song shall be, Ho - san - na to our King;

His praise to whom their souls be-long, Let all the chil-dren sing.
Till morn and eve, and noon to night, And heav'n to earth re - ply.
This is the chil-dren's ju - bi-lee, Let all the chil - dren sing.

LIKE AN ARMY WE ARE MARCHING.

SALLIE MARTIN. WM. J. KIRKPATRICK.

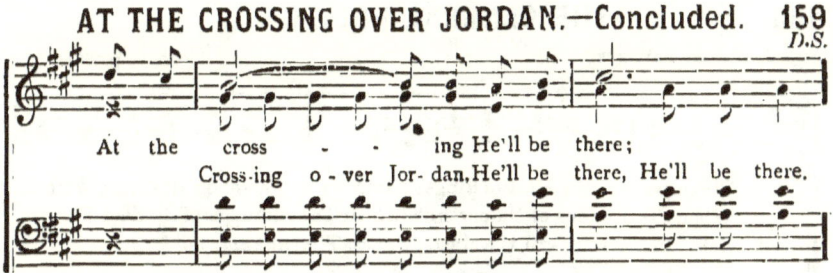

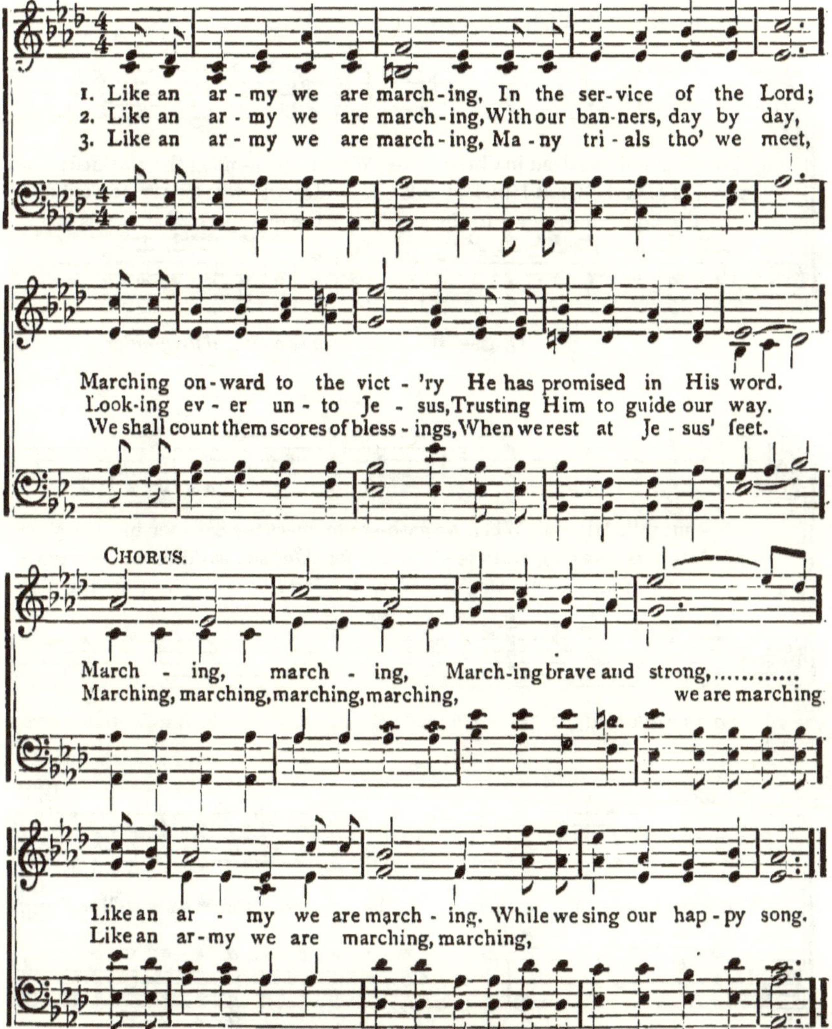

THE GENERAL ROLL CALL.

J. W. Van DeVenter.   W. S. Weeden.

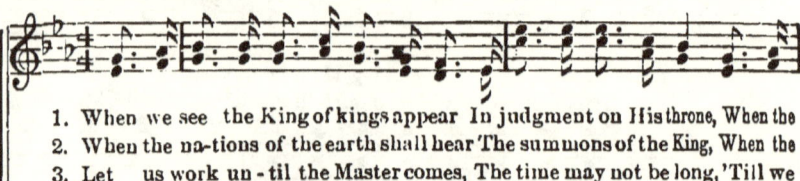

1. When we see the King of kings appear In judgment on His throne, When the
2. When the na-tions of the earth shall hear The summons of the King, When the
3. Let us work un-til the Master comes, The time may not be long, 'Till we

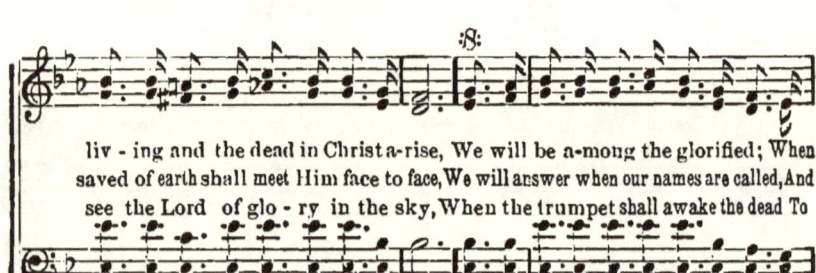

liv-ing and the dead in Christ a-rise, We will be a-mong the glorified; When
saved of earth shall meet Him face to face, We will answer when our names are called, And
see the Lord of glo-ry in the sky, When the trumpet shall awake the dead To

D. S.—*When our names are read up yonder, From the*

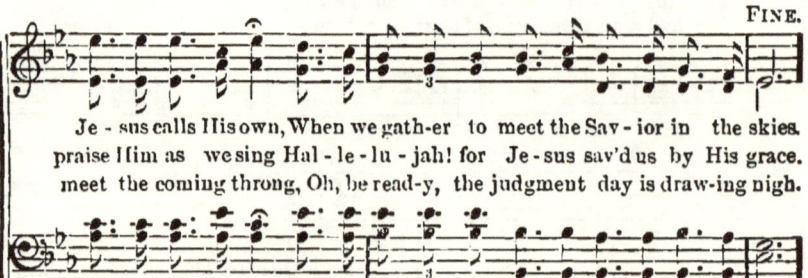

Je-sus calls His own, When we gath-er to meet the Sav-ior in the skies.
praise Him as we sing Hal-le-lu-jah! for Je-sus sav'd us by His grace.
meet the coming throng, Oh, be read-y, the judgment day is draw-ing nigh.

pages white and fair, When the gen-er-al roll is called, we'll all be there.

CHORUS.   **D. S.**

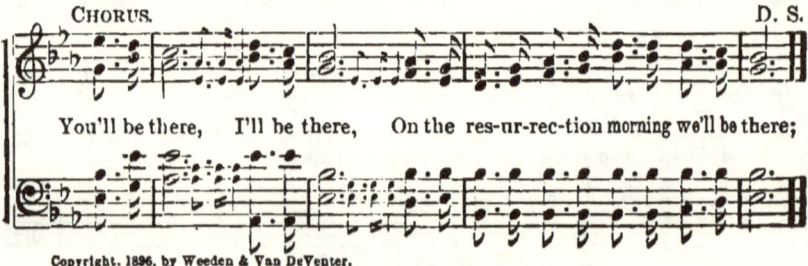

You'll be there, I'll be there, On the res-ur-rec-tion morning we'll be there;

Copyright, 1896, by Weeden & Van DeVenter.

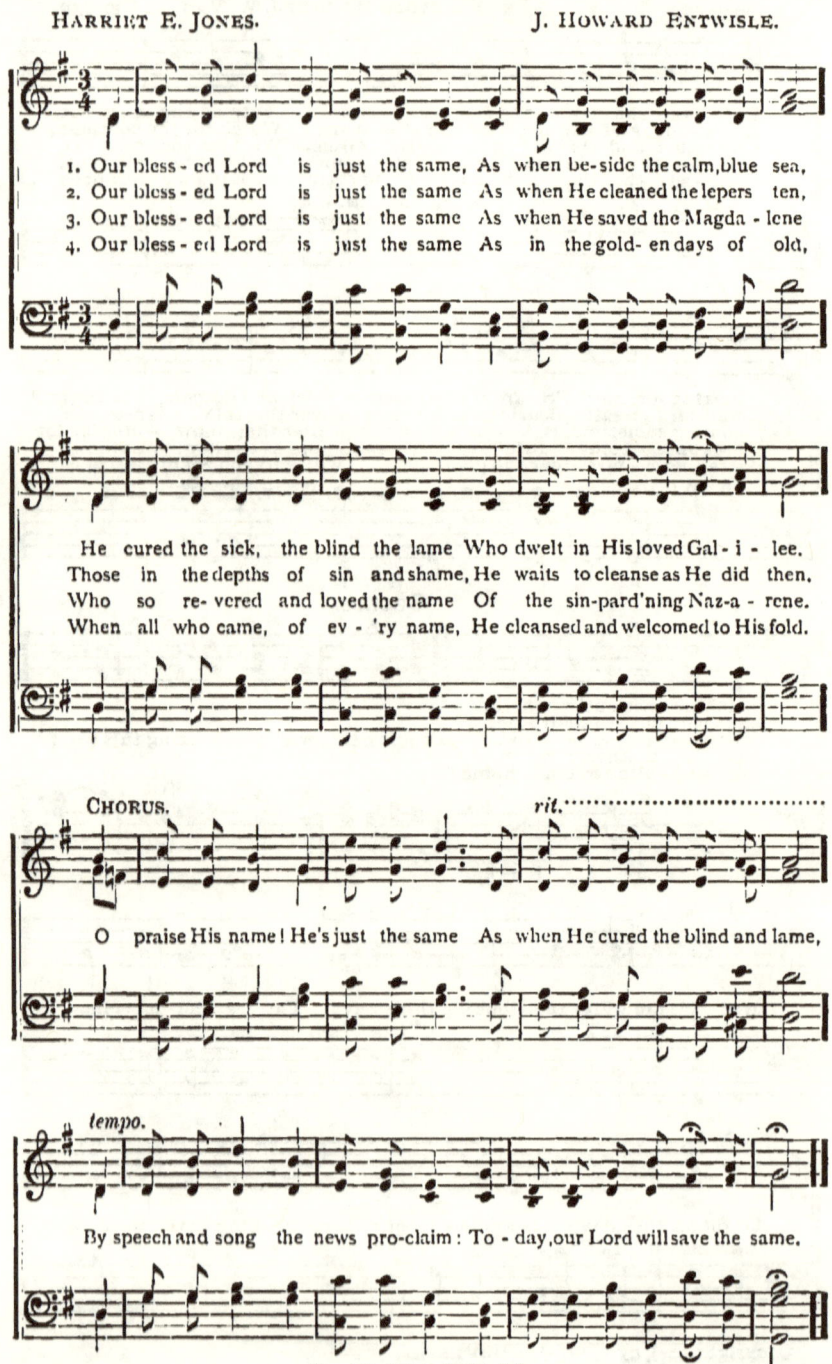

THE LIGHTS OF HOME.—Concluded.

There,...... beyond the bil-lows' foam, We see the lights of home.
There, be-yond, be-yond

JESUS TOUCHED MY HEART.

IDA SCOTT TAYLOR.   J. S. FEARIS.

1. Je-sus touch'd my sin - ful heart, Bade my tears re - pent - ant start,
2. Je-sus touch'd my sin - ful heart, Bade me walk with him a - part,
3. Je-sus touch'd my sin - ful heart, Bade my e - vil tho'ts de - part,
4. Je-sus touch'd my sin - ful heart, Bade me choose the bet - ter part,

Showed me all my guilt and sin, Made me clean and pure with - in.
Stooped my lamp of faith to trim, Made me feel my need of him.
Soft - ly whis-pered in my ear Ten-der words of hope and cheer.
Led me gen - tly to his breast, Fill'd my soul with peace and rest.

CHORUS.

Jesus touch'd my heart with his pow'r divine, His pow'r divine, his pow'r divine;

Jesus touch'd my heart with his pow'r divine; I'm happy since his love is mine.

Copyright, 1897, by Wm. J. Kirkpatrick.

168. WE PASS THIS WAY BUT ONCE.

AMANDA R. MEUSCH.   FRANK M. DAVIS, by per.

1. As we jour-ney on our pathway, Which thro' life's great valley leads;
2. Let us help the wea-ry pilgrim, Whom we meet up-on our way,
3. Let us not de-lay our actions, Thoughtless for an-oth-er day;

Let us scat-ter seeds of kindness, Strew our path with lov-ing deeds.
With a kind-ly word and ac-tion, With a lov-ing deed to-day.
There are souls that must be rescued, Let us help them while we may.

CHORUS.

We pass . . . . . this way but once, We
We pass this way, this way but once,

pass . . . . . this way but once; Let us
We pass this way, this way but once; Let us

scat-ter seeds of kindness, For we pass this way but once.
scatter seeds of kindness, scatter seeds of kindness,

Copyright, 1890, by Frank M. Davis.

170 WELCOME FOR ME.

FANNY J. CROSBY.   WM. J. KIRKPATRICK.

1. Like a bird on the deep, far a-way from its nest, I had wander'd, my Sav-iour, from Thee; But Thy dear lov-ing voice call'd me home to Thy breast, And I knew there was wel-come for me.
2. I am safe in the ark, I have fold-ed my wings On the bos-om of mer-cy di-vine; I am fill'd with the light of Thy pres-ence so bright, And the joy that will ev-er be mine.
3. I am safe in the ark, and I dread not the storm, Tho a-round me the sur-ges may roll; I will look to the skies, where the day nev-er dies, I will sing of the joy in my soul.

CHORUS.

Welcome for me, Sav-iour, from Thee; A smile and a welcome for me: Now, like a dove, I rest in Thy love, And find a sweet ref-uge in Thee.
in Thee.

Copyright, 1885, by W. J. Kirkpatrick.

STEPPING IN THE LIGHT.

L. H. EDMUNDS.   WM. J. KIRKPATRICK.

1. Try-ing to walk in the steps of the Sav-iour, Try-ing to fol-low our
2. Press-ing more closely to Him who is lead-ing, When we are tempt-ed to
3. Walk-ing in foot-steps of gen-tle forbearance, Foot-steps of faith-ful-ness,
4. Try-ing to walk in the steps of the Sav-iour, Up-ward, still up-ward we'll

Copyright, 1890, by Wm. J. Kirkpatrick.

STEPPING IN THE LIGHT.—Concluded. 171

Sav - iour and King; Shap - ing our lives by His bless - ed ex - am - ple,
turn from the way; Trust - ing the arm that is strong to de - fend us,
mer - cy, and love, Look - ing to Him for the grace free - ly prom - ised,
fol - low our Guide, When we shall see Him, "the King in His beau - ty,"

CHORUS.

Hap-py, how hap-py, the songs that we bring.
Hap-py, how hap-py, our prais - es each day.
Hap-py, how hap-py, our jour - ney a - bove.
Hap-py, how hap-py, our place at His side.
} How beautiful to walk in the

steps of the Sav - iour, Stepping in the light, Stepping in the light; How

beau - ti - ful to walk in the steps of the Saviour, Led in paths of light.

HE CAME TO SAVE ME.

H. E. BLAIR.   WM. J. KIRKPATRICK.

1. { When Je - sus laid His crown aside, He came to save me;
     When on the cross He bled and died,............ He came to save me.
2. { In my poor heart He deigns to dwell, He came to save me;
     O, praise His name, I know it well,............ He came to save me.

CHORUS.

I'm so glad, I'm so glad, I'm so glad that Jesus came, And grace is free,
He............ came to save me.

3 With gentle hand He leads me still,
   He came to save me;
  And trusting Him I fear no ill,
   He came to save me.

4 To Him my faith with rapture clings,
   He came to save me;
  To Him my heart looks up and sings,
   He came to save me.

Copyright, 1885, by Wm. J. Kirkpatrick.

172 WHAT REJOICING THERE WILL BE.

Mrs. Harriet E. Jones.   J. Howard Entwisle.

Slow, and with great expression.

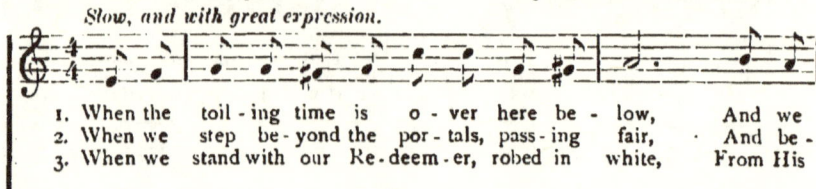

1. When the toil-ing time is o-ver here be-low, And we
2. When we step be-yond the por-tals, pass-ing fair, · And be-
3. When we stand with our Re-deem-er, robed in white, From His

rise to that sweet home with light a-glow— And a-mid the bright im-
hold the ma-ny mansions wait-ing there— Homes of beau-ty that shall
hand our crowns re-ceiv-ing, crowns of light, Which He purchased on the

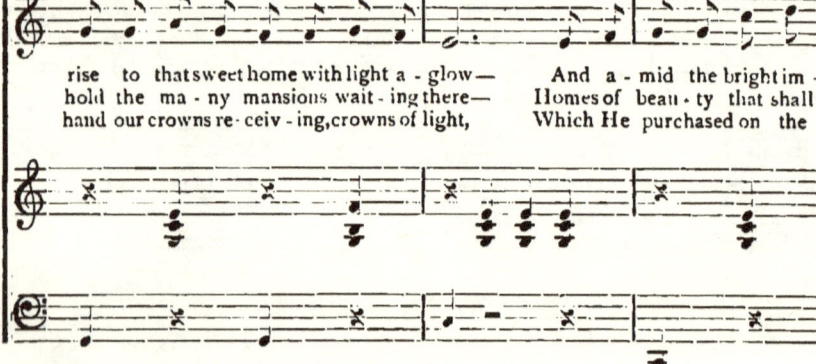

mortals, loved ones see,......What a shout, O what re-joic-ing there will be.
stand e-ter-nal-ly........What a shout, O what re-joic-ing there will be.
cross of Cal-va-ry........What a shout, O what re-joic-ing there will be.

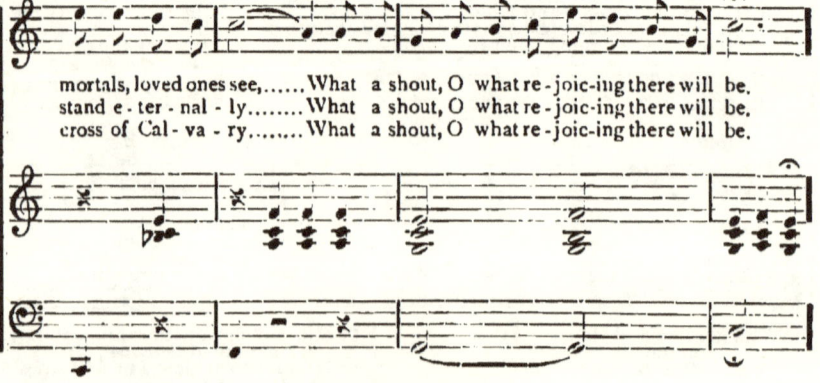

Copyright, 1897, by Hall-Mack Co.

What Rejoicing There Will Be. Concluded. 173

RUEBUSH. 7s.

Frank L. Armstrong.

1. Lord of hosts, how love-ly fair, E'en on earth Thy tem-ples are;
2. From Thy gra-cious pres-ence flows Bliss that soft-ens all our woes;
3. Here we sup-pli-cate Thy throne, Here Thou mak'st Thy glo-ries known;
4. Thus with sa-cred songs of joy, We our hap-py lives em-ploy;

Here Thy wait-ing peo-ple see Much of heav'n and much of Thee.
While Thy Spir-it's ho-ly fire Warms our hearts with pure de-sire.
Here we learn Thy right-eous ways, Taste Thy love and sing Thy praise.
Love, and long to love Thee more, Till from earth to heav'n we soar.

GATHERING SHEAVES FOR JESUS.—Concluded. 175

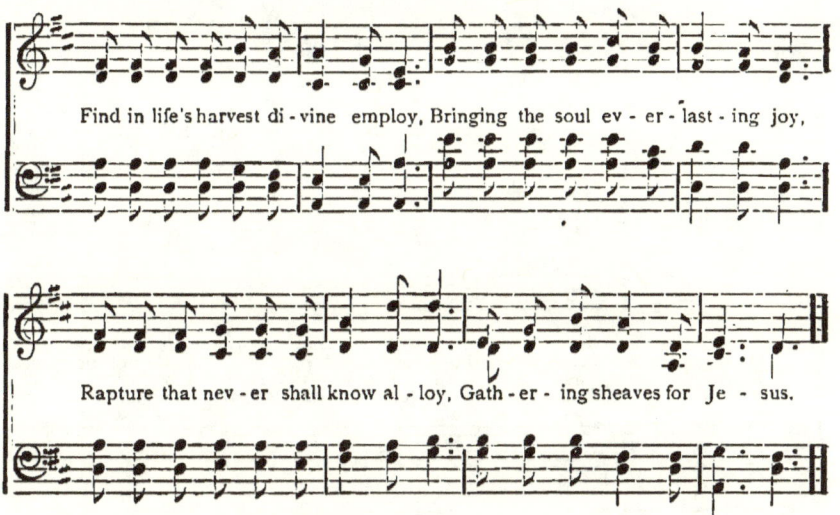

JUST AS I AM.

CHARLOTTE ELLIOTT.   (WOODWORTH. L. M.)   WM. B. BRADBURY.

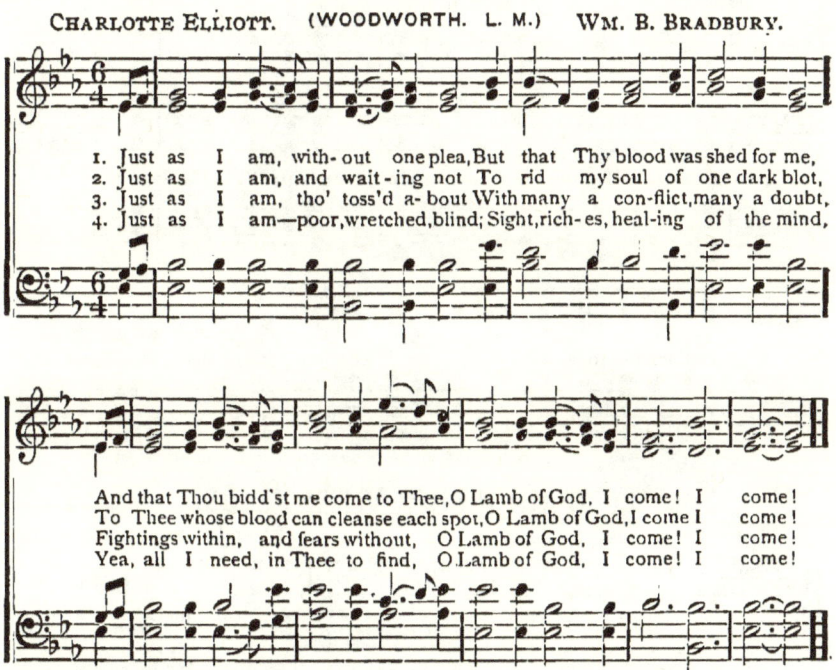

1. Just as I am, with-out one plea, But that Thy blood was shed for me,
2. Just as I am, and wait-ing not To rid my soul of one dark blot,
3. Just as I am, tho' toss'd a-bout With many a con-flict, many a doubt,
4. Just as I am—poor, wretched, blind; Sight, rich-es, heal-ing of the mind,

And that Thou bidd'st me come to Thee, O Lamb of God, I come! I come!
To Thee whose blood can cleanse each spot, O Lamb of God, I come! I come!
Fightings within, and fears without, O Lamb of God, I come! I come!
Yea, all I need, in Thee to find, O Lamb of God, I come! I come!

5 Just as I am Thou wilt receive,
 Wilt welcome, pardon, cleanse, relieve;
 Because Thy promise I believe,
 O Lamb of God, I come! I come!

6 Just as I am—Thy love unknown
 Hath broken every barrier down;
 Now, to be Thine, yea, Thine alone,
 O Lamb of God, I come! I come!

176 HE HIDETH MY SOUL.

FANNY J. CROSBY.
Allegretto.
WM. J. KIRKPATRICK.

1. A won-der-ful Sav-iour is Je-sus my Lord, A won-der-ful Sav-iour to me,
2. A won-der-ful Sav-iour is Je-sus my Lord, He tak-eth my bur-den a-way,
3. With num-ber-less bless-ings each mo-ment He crowns, And fill'd with His ful-ness di-vine,
4. When clothed in His bright-ness trans-port-ed I rise To meet Him in clouds of the sky,

He hid-eth my soul in the cleft of the rock,
He hold-eth me up, and I shall not be moved,
I sing in my rap-ture, O, glo-ry to God
His per-fect sal-va-tion, His won-der-ful love,

CHORUS.

Where riv-ers of pleasure I see.
He giv-eth me strength as my day.
For such a Redeem-er as mine.
I'll shout with the millions on high.

He hid-eth my soul in the cleft of the rock, That shadows a dry, thirsty land; He hid-eth my life in the depths of His love, And cov-ers me there with His hand, And cov-ers me there with His hand.

Copyright, 1890, by Wm. J. Kirkpatrick.

COMPANIONSHIP WITH JESUS.

MARY D. JAMES.
WM. J. KIRKPATRICK.

1. Oh, bless-ed fel-low-ship di-vine! Oh, joy supremely sweet! Com-
2. I'm walk-ing close to Je-sus' side; So close that I can hear The
3. I'm lean-ing on His lov-ing breast, A-long life's wea-ry way; My
4. I know His shelt'ring wings of love Are al-ways o'er me spread; And

Copyright, 1875, by Wm. J. Kirkpatrick.

ONE THING I KNOW. 179

E. E. HEWITT.
WM. J. KIRKPATRICK.

SOLO OR QUARTET.

1. One thing I know;......... O bless his name,......... To me the Lord............. of mer-cy
2. One thing I know;......... He heard my cries,...... With mighty power...He touched my
3. One thing I know;.........He died for me,............In Him my hope,......my trust shall
4. One thing I know;......... the Saviour's mine,.........O boundless grace,.........O joy di-
5. One thing I know;......... O help me sing............Such happy praise.........to Christ our

One thing I know;   O bless his name,   To me the Lord

came,............ He filled my heart............with love's bright flame,......... This I
eyes,.............. To see the light............that nev-er dies,............. This I
be,................ My Sav-iour lives............... e-ter-nal-ly............... This I
vine!............ And heavenly beams........... around me shine,............ This I
King............ While smiling faith........... and love up springs,........... This I

of mer-cy came,   He filled my heart   with love's bright flame,

CHORUS.

know,................ this I know. I know, I know,............... He loved me

This I know,   I know, I know,

so,................ He saved my soul............from sin and woe,...............Now peace and

He love me so,   He saved my soul   from sin and woe,

joy............ He doth be-stow,............. This I know,............this I know.

Now peace and joy   He doth bestow,   This I know,

Copyright, 1891, by Wm. J. Kirkpatrick.

MEET IN THE MORNING.—Concluded.

We are pressing forward to the golden strand, Where joy will crown us in the morning.
O, the time is coming, we shall soon be there, And joy will crown us in the morning.
Where our friends are waiting, at the gate of life, And joy will crown us in the morning.

CHORUS.
In the morning, in the morning, We will gather with the faithful in the morning;
Where the night of sorrow shall be rolled away, And joy will crown us in the morning.

4 Where the hills are blooming on the other shore,
We'll meet each other in the morning;
Where the heart's deep longing will be felt no more,
And joy will crown us in the morning.

5 In the boundless rapture of a Saviour's love,
We'll meet each other in the morning;
Then we'll sing His glory in the realms above,
And joy will crown us in the morning.

I'LL BE THERE.

ISAAC WATTS.   Adapted by WM. J. KIRKPATRICK.

1. { There is a land of pure delight, Where saints immortal reign; }
   { In fi-nite day ex-cludes the night, And pleasures banish pain. }
2. { There ev-er-last-ing spring abides, And nev-er with'ring flow'rs; }
   { Death, like a narrow sea, divides This heav'nly land from ours. }

CHORUS.
I'll be there, I'll be there. When the first trumpet sounds I'll be there,
   I'll be there, I'll be there.   I'll be there,
I'll be there, I'll be there, When the first trumpet sounds I'll be there.
   I'll be there, I'll be there,

Copyright, 1887, by Wm. J. Kirkpatrick.

3 Sweet fields beyond the swelling flood
Stand dressed in living green;
So to the Jews old Canaan stood,
While Jordan rolled between.

4 Could we but climb where Moses stood,
And view the landscape o'er,
Not Jordan's stream, nor death's cold flood
Should fright us from the shore.

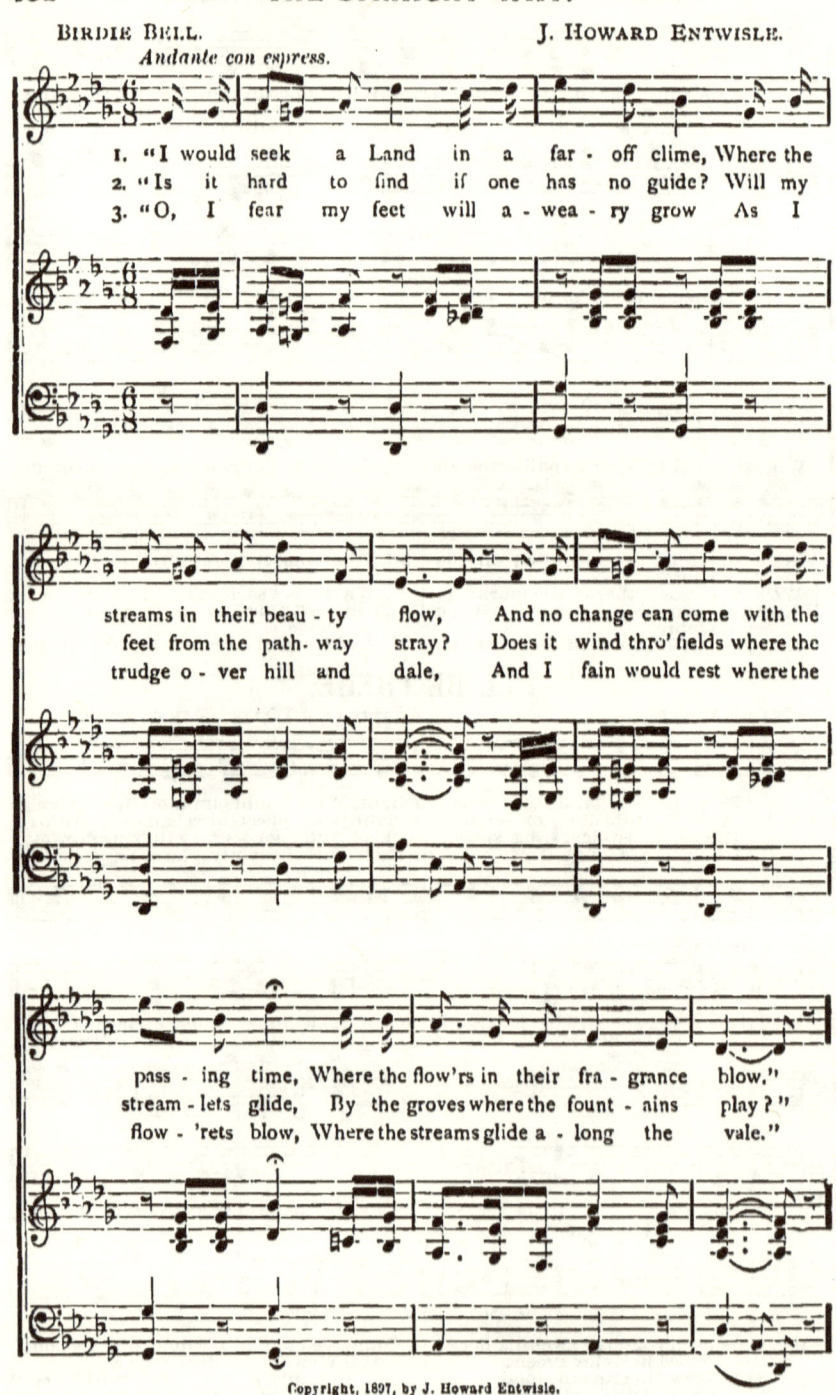

ONLY A FEW BRIEF YEARS.

IDA L. REED. J. HOWARD ENTWISLE.

Feelingly.

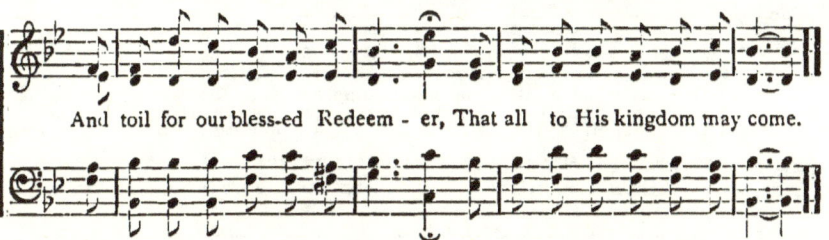

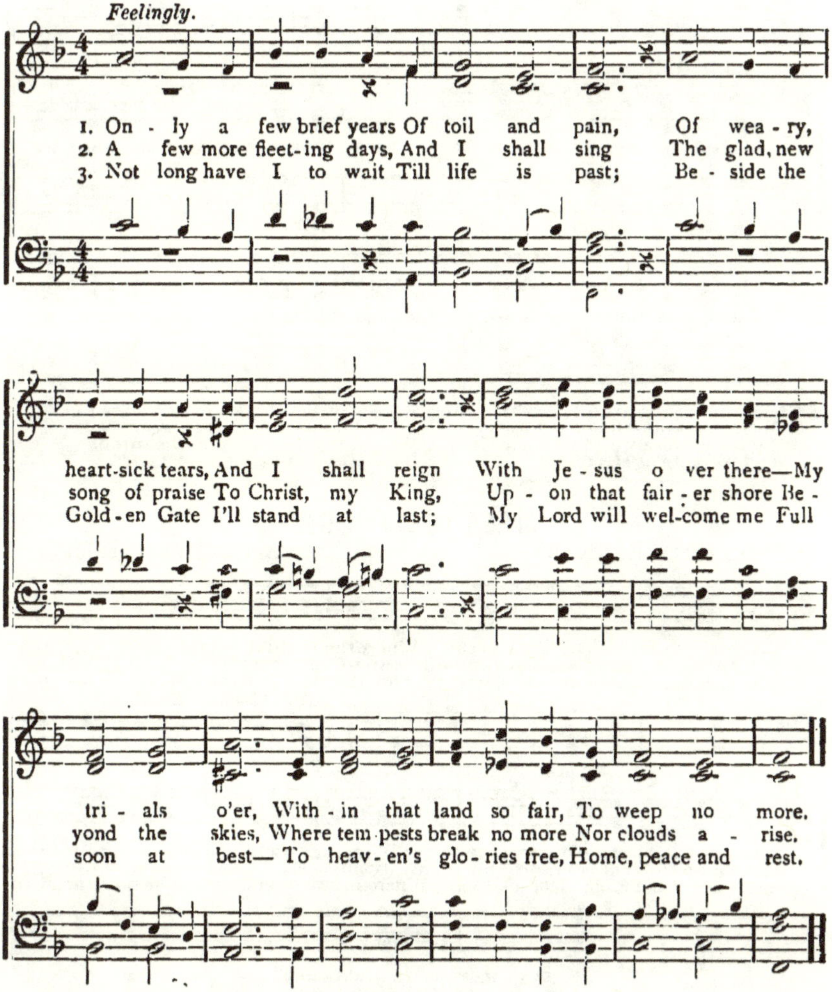

BLESSED BE THE NAME.

W. H. CLARK. Arr. by WM. J. KIRKPATRICK.

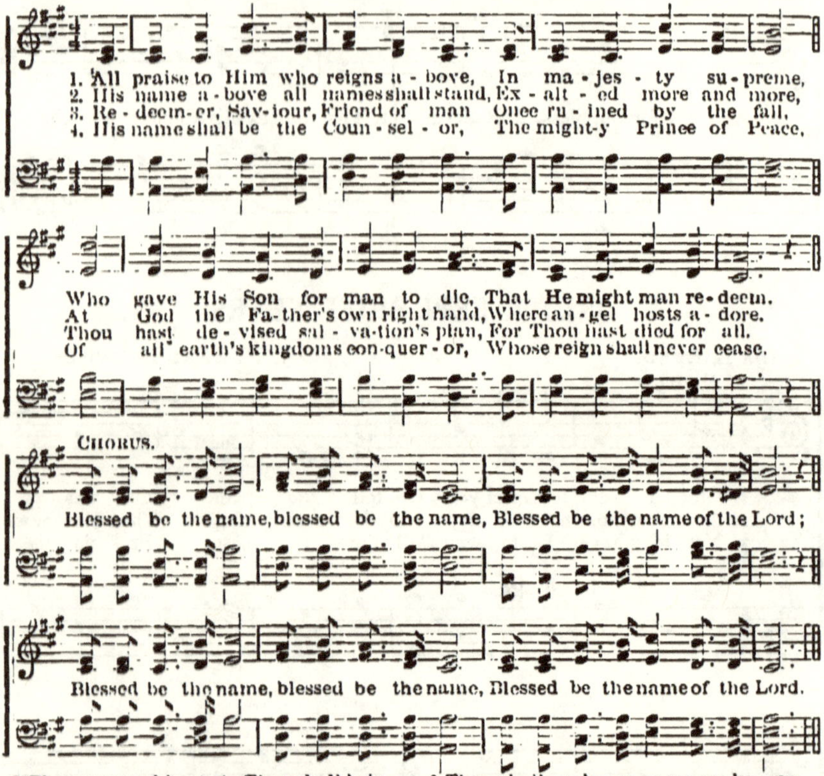

5 The ransomed hosts to Thee shall bring
Their praise and homage meet;
With rapturous awe adore their King,
And worship at His feet.

6 Then shall we know as we are known,
And in that world above
Forever sing around the throne
His everlasting love.

MEET ME THERE.

HENRIETTA E. BLAIR. WM. J. KIRKPATRICK.

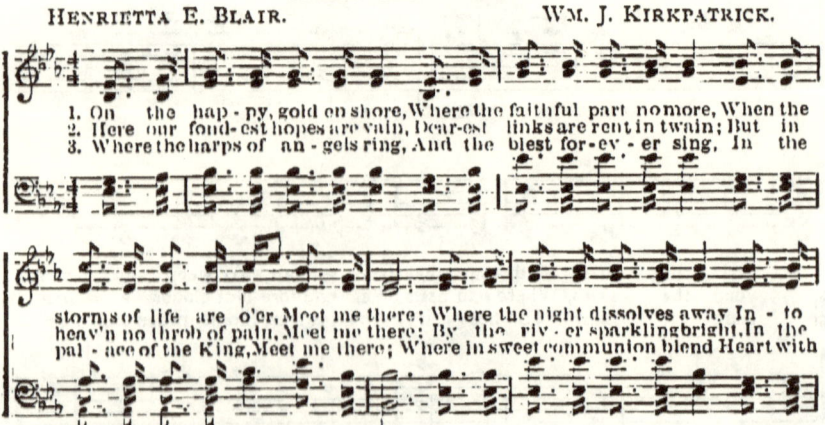

MEET ME THERE.—Concluded.

pure and per-fect day, I am go-ing home to stay, Meet me there.
cit - y of de - light, Where our faith is lost in sight, Meet me there.
heart, and friend with friend, In a world that ne'er shall end, Meet me there.

D.S.—hap-py gold - en shore, Where the faithful part no more, Meet me there.

CHORUS.
Meet me there, meet me there, Where the tree of life is
Meet me there, meet me there,

blooming, Meet me there; When the storms of life are o'er, On the
Meet me there;

Copyright, 1885, by Wm. J. Kirkpatrick.

HALLELUJAH! AMEN.

HENRIETTA E. BLAIR.   Adapted and arr. by WM. J. KIRKPATRICK.

1. How oft in ho-ly converse With Christ, my Lord alone, I seem to hear the
2. They pass'd thro' toils and trials, And tho' the strife was long, They share the victor's
3. My soul takes up the cho - rus, And press-ing on my way, Commun-ing still with
4. Thro' grace I soon shall conquer, And reach my home on high; And thro' e-ter-nal

CHORUS.
mil - lions That sing around His throne;
con-quest, And sing the vic-tor's song.   } Hal-le - lu-jah, A - men, Hal-le -
Je - sus, I sing from day to day.
a - ges I'll shout beyond the sky.

poco ritard.
lu-jah, A - men. Hal - le - lu - jah, A - men. A - men, A - men.

Copyright, 1885, by Wm. J. Kirkpatrick.

194. 'TIS SO SWEET TO TRUST IN JESUS.

Mrs. LOUISA M. R. STEAD.   WM. J. KIRKPATRICK.

1. "Tis so sweet to trust in Je - sus, Just to take Him at His Word;
2. O, how sweet to trust in Je - sus, Just to trust His cleans-ing blood;
3. Yes, 'tis sweet to trust in Je - sus, Just from sin and self to cease;
4. I'm so glad I learn'd to trust Thee, Pre-cious Je - sus, Saviour, Friend;

Just to rest up - on His prom-ise; Just to know, "Thus saith the Lord."
Just in sim - ple faith to plunge me 'Neath the heal - ing, cleansing flood.
Just from Je - sus sim - ply tak - ing Life, and rest, and joy, and peace.
And I know that Thou art with me, Wilt be with me to the end.

CHORUS.

Je - sus, Je - sus, how I trust Him; How I've prov'd Him o'er and o'er.

Je - sus, Je - sus, Pre - cious Je - sus! O for grace to trust Him more.

Copyright, 1882, by Wm. J. Kirkpatrick.

CALMLY LEANING ON MY SAVIOUR.

E. E. HEWITT.   WM. J. KIRKPATRICK.

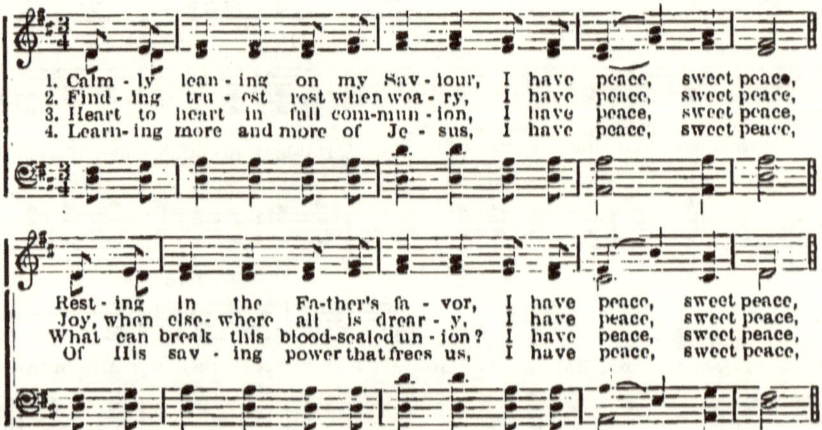

1. Calm - ly lean - ing on my Sav - iour, I have peace, sweet peace,
2. Find - ing tru - est rest when wea - ry, I have peace, sweet peace,
3. Heart to heart in full com-mun - ion, I have peace, sweet peace,
4. Learn - ing more and more of Je - sus, I have peace, sweet peace,

Rest - ing in the Fa-ther's fa - vor, I have peace, sweet peace,
Joy, when else - where all is drear - y, I have peace, sweet peace,
What can break this blood-sealed un - ion? I have peace, sweet peace,
Of His sav - ing power that frees us, I have peace, sweet peace,

Copyright, 1887, by Wm. J. Kirkpatrick.

CALMLY LEANING ON MY SAVIOUR.—Concluded. 195

Tho' the storm-waves roll a-round me, Naught of ter-ror shall confound me,
Here the hap-py se-cret know-ing, Se-cret of the Lord's own showing.
All my wants to Him con-fid-ing, In His blest pa-vil-ion hid-ing,
Hum-bly now His grace con-fess-ing, His own prom-ised gift pos-sess-ing,

ad lib.

While these arms of might sur-round me, I have peace, sweet peace.
Grace for grace, His love be-stow-ing, I have peace, sweet peace.
In His change-less love a-bid-ing, I have peace, sweet peace.
To His name be end-less bless-ing, I have peace, sweet peace.

ENTIRE CONSECRATION.

FRANCES R. HAVERGAL. (Chorus by W. J. K.) WM. J. KIRKPATRICK.

1. Take my life, and let it be Con-se-cra-ted, Lord, to Thee;
2. Take my feet, and let them be Swift and beau-ti-ful for Thee;
3. Take my lips, and let them be Filled with mes-sa-ges for Thee;
4. Take my moments, and my days, Let them flow in end-less praise;

Take my hands and let them move At the im-pulse of Thy love.
Take my voice, and let me sing Al-ways, on-ly for my King.
Take my sil-ver and my gold,— Not a mite would I with-hold.
Take my in-tel-lect, and use Ev-'ry pow'r as Thou shalt choose.

CHORUS.

{ Wash me in the Saviour's precious blood, the pre-cious blood,
{ Cleanse me in its pu-ri-fy-ing flood, the heal-ing flood, } Lord, I give to

Thee my life and all, to be Thine, henceforth e-ter-nal-ly.

5 Take my will, and make it Thine;
It shall be no longer mine;
Take my heart,—it is Thine own,—
It shall be Thy royal throne.

6 Take my love,—my Lord, I pour
At Thy feet its treasure-store!
Take myself, and I will be
Ever, only, all for Thee!

Copyright, 1875, by Wm. J. Kirkpatrick.

There's a Beautiful Heavenly Country.—Concluded. 197

Fair land of heaven thy praises we sing, Tell-ing the sto-ry of Jesus our King;

Beautiful country, heavenly country, There we shall dwell with the ransom'd throng.

LOVE DIVINE.

CHARLES WESLEY.

1. Love di-vine, all love ex-cel-ling, Joy of heav'n, to earth come down!
Fix in us Thy humble dwell-ing! All thy faith-ful mer-cies crown.
D.S.—Vis-it us with Thy sal-va-tion; En-ter ev-'ry trembling heart.
Je-sus, thou art all com-pas-sion, Pure, un-bound-ed love Thou art;

2 Breathe, oh, breathe Thy loving Spirit
   Into every troubled breast!
   Let us all in Thee inherit,
   Let us find that second rest.
Take away our bent to sinning;
   Alpha and Omega be;
End of faith, as its beginning,
   Set our hearts at liberty.

3 Finish then Thy new creation;
   Pure and spotless let us be;
Let us see Thy great salvation,
   Perfectly restored in Thee:
Changed from glory into glory,
   'Till in heaven we take our place,
Till we cast our crowns before Thee,
   Lost in wonder, love, and praise.

BEAUTIFUL ROBES. Concluded.

Walk-ing with Je-sus in white, Beau-ti-ful robes we shall wear.

JESUS FOR ME.

W. J. K. W. J. KIRKPATRICK.

1. Je-sus, my Sav-iour, is all things to me, O, what a Won-der-ful
2. Je-sus, in sick-ness, and Je-sus in health, Je-sus in pov-er-ty,
3. He is my Ref-uge, my Rock and my Tow'r, He is my For-tress, my
4. He is my Pro-phet, my Priest and my King, He is my Bread of Life
5. Je-sus in sor-row, in joy, or in pain, Je-sus my Treasure in

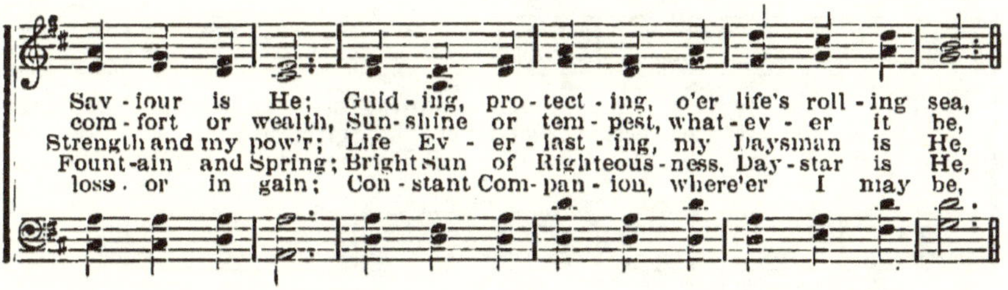

Sav-iour is He; Guid-ing, pro-tect-ing, o'er life's roll-ing sea,
com-fort or wealth, Sun-shine or tem-pest, what-ev-er it be,
Strength and my pow'r; Life Ev-er-last-ing, my Daysman is He,
Fount-ain and Spring; Bright Sun of Righteous-ness, Day-star is He,
loss or in gain; Con-stant Com-pan-ion, where'er I may be,

CHORUS.

Might-y De-liv-'rer— Je-sus for me. Je-sus for me,
He is my safe-ty:— Je-sus for me.
Bless-ed Re-deem-er— Je-sus for me.
Horn of Sal-va-tion— Je-sus for me.
Liv-ing or dy-ing— Je-sus for me!

Je-sus for me, All the time, ev-'ry-where, Je-sus for me.

Copyright, 1885, by Wm. J. Kirkpatrick.

WE'LL SING HIS WONDERFUL LOVE.—Concluded. 201

He triumph'd o-ver sin and the grave, And reigneth for-ev-er-more.

IN THE HOUR OF TRIAL.

JAMES MONTGOMERY.   SPENCER LANE.

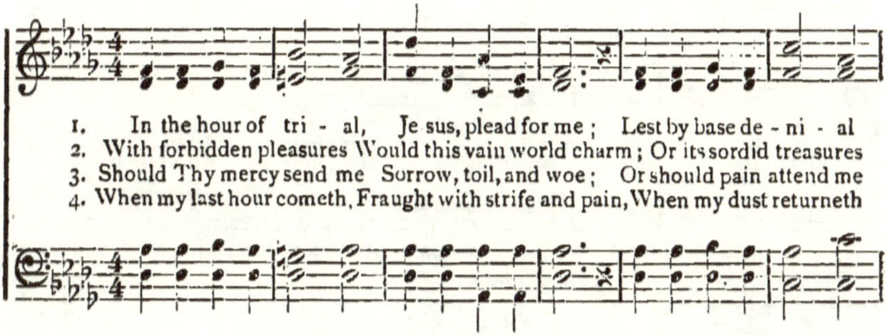

1. In the hour of tri - al, Je sus, plead for me ; Lest by base de - ni - al
2. With forbidden pleasures Would this vain world charm; Or its sordid treasures
3. Should Thy mercy send me Sorrow, toil, and woe ; Or should pain attend me
4. When my last hour cometh, Fraught with strife and pain, When my dust returneth

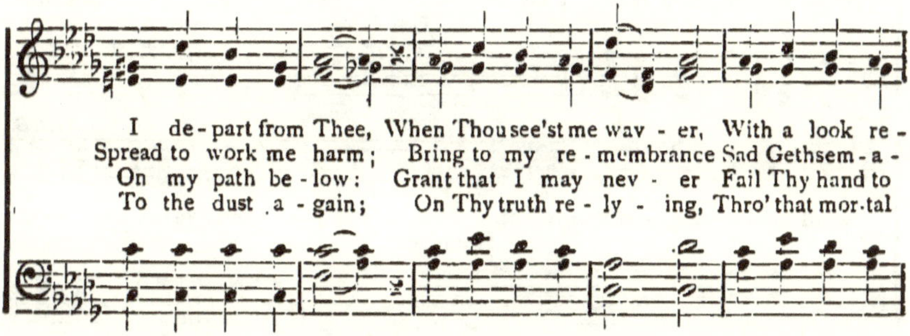

I de-part from Thee, When Thou see'st me wav - er, With a look re -
Spread to work me harm; Bring to my re - membrance Sad Gethsem - a -
On my path be - low; Grant that I may nev - er Fail Thy hand to
To the dust a - gain; On Thy truth re - ly - ing, Thro' that mor-tal

call,   Nor for fear or fa - vor Suf - fer me to fall.
ne,   Or, in dark - er semblance, Cross-crown'd Calva - ry.
see;   Grant that I may ev - er Cast my care on Thee.
strife,   Je - sus, take me, dy - ing, To e - ter - nal life.

202 PASS IT ON.

Rev. Henry Burton, A. M.   Wm. J. Kirkpatrick.

1. Have you had a kind-ness shown? Pass it on, pass it on! 'Twas not
2. Did you hear the lov-ing word? Pass it on, pass it on! Like the
3. Have you found the heaven-ly light? Pass it on, pass it on! Souls are

given for thee a-lone, Pass it on, pass it on! Let it trav-el down the
sing-ing of a bird? Pass it on, pass it on! Let its mu-sic live and
grop-ing in the night, Day-light gone, Day-light gone! Hold your lighted lamp on

years, Let it wipe an-oth-er's tears; Till in heaven the deed ap-pears,
grow, Let it cheer an-oth-er's woe; You have reaped what oth-ers sow,
high, Be a star in some one's sky, He may live who else would die.

D. S.—Christ, you live a-gain, Live for him, with him you reign.

Fine. CHORUS.

Pass it on, pass it on! Pass it on, pass it on! Cheer-ful
Pass it on, pass it on!

D. S.

word or lov-ing deed, Pass it on, Live for self, you live in vain; Live for
Pass it on,

Copyright, 1888, by Wm. J. Kirkpatrick.

CALVARY'S STREAM IS FLOWING.

Lidie H. Edmunds.   Adapted and Arr. by Wm. J. Kirkpatrick.

1. From that dear cross where Je - sus died, Cal-v'ry's stream is flow-ing;
2. Come, wash the stain of sin a - way, Cal-v'ry's stream is flow-ing;
3. For ev - 'ry con - trite, wounded soul, Cal-v'ry's stream is flow-ing;
4. For ev - 'ry wea - ry, ach - ing heart, Cal-v'ry's stream is flow-ing;
5. With life and peace up - on its tide, Cal-v'ry's stream is flow-ing.

Copyright, 1891, by Wm. J. Kirkpatrick.

CALVARY'S STREAM IS FLOWING.—Concluded. 203

From bleeding hands and feet and side, Cal-v'ry's stream is flow-ing.
Come, while 'tis call'd sal-va-tion's day, Cal-v'ry's stream is flow-ing.
Step in just now, and be made whole, Cal-v'ry's stream is flow-ing.
A ten-der heal-ing to im-part, Cal-v'ry's stream is flow-ing.
Sweet bless-ings down the a-ges glide, Cal-v'ry's stream is flow-ing.

CHORUS.

Cal-v'ry's stream is flow-ing, Cal-v'ry's stream is flow-ing;
Flow-ing so free for you and for me, Cal-v'ry's stream is flow-ing.

HEAVEN IS MY HOME.

THOS. R. TAYLOR.   Scotch air.

1. I'm but a stran-ger here, Heaven is my home; Earth is a
2. What though the tem-pest rage, Heaven is my home; Short is my
3. There at my Sav-iour's side, Heaven is my home; I shall be

des-ert drear, Heaven is my home. Danger and sorrow stand, Round me on
pil-grimage, Heaven is my home. Time's cold and wintry blast, Soon will be
glo-ri-fied, Heaven is my home. There are the good and blest, Those I loved

ev-'ry hand, Heav'n is my fa-ther-land, Heav'n is my home.
o-ver-past, I shall reach home at last, Heav'n is my home.
most and best, There, too, I soon shall rest, Heav'n is my home.

IT JUST SUITS ME.—Concluded.

Far ex-cel the grand-est knowledge Of the ser-a-phim in light;
To the sparkling, liv-ing wa-ters Flow-ing ful-ly, free-ly still;
For the grace of our Re-deem-er Must our high-est thought ex-ceed;
Can we ev-er praise Him right-ly? Tell how grace and glo-ry blend?

I can nev-er, nev-er fath-om Half its ho-ly mys-te-ry,
No, I know not why He loves me, But His blood is all my plea;
To the might-y, roy-al storehouse Let me use the gol-den key,
Now the Prince of Peace is reign-ing, O-ver-rul-ing all I see;

CHORUS.

But I know it is for sin-ners, And it just suits me. It just suits
I can trust His "who-so-ev-er," For it just suits me.
Find the spe-cial, ten-der promise That will just suit me.
So, what-ev-er lot He or-ders, May it just suit me.

me, It just suits me, This won-der-ful sal-va-tion, It just suits me.

THERE YOU'LL SING HALLELUJAH.

CHO.—There you'll sing hal-le-lu-jah, And I'll sing hal-le-lu-jah,
And we'll all sing hal-le-lu-jah, In that bright world a-bove.

1 On Jordan's stormy banks I stand,
  And cast a wishful eye
To Canaan's fair and happy land,
  Where my possessions lie.

2 O the transporting, rapturous scene,
  That rises to my sight!
Sweet fields arrayed in living green,
  And rivers of delight.

3 When shall I reach that happy place,
  And be forever blest?
When shall I see my Father's face,
  And in His bosom rest?

4 Fill'd with delight, my raptured soul
  Would here no longer stay;
Though Jordan's waves around me roll,
  Fearless I'd launch away.

208. WHEN THE CURTAINS ARE LIFTED.

Mrs. ANNIE WITTENMYER. WM. J. KIRKPATRICK.

1. When the cur-tains are lift-ed, Oh, what shall I see? Will my Lord with His an-gels Be wait-ing for me? Will He wel-come my com-ing, And crown me His own, With the saints of all a-ges, That cir-cle His throne?
2. Will the heav-en-ly cit-y burst full on my sight; And the throne of His glo-ry, That giv-eth it light; Will the feet torn and wea-ry Reach pavements of gold, And the eyes red with weeping The Sav-iour be-hold?
3. Now the fu-ture is hid-den, I see but a pace, Yet it may be I'm near-ing The end of the race; It will mat-ter but lit-tle What chang-es may come, If my Lord with His an-gels Shall welcome me home.
4. When His glo-ri-fied presence Shall gladden mine eyes, I'll be changed and be like Him, And with Him a-rise; And the hands hard with la-bor A vic-tor's palm raise; And the lips tuned to sor-row Sing anthems of praise.

CHORUS.

(1,2,3.) When the cur-tains are lift-ed, Oh, what shall I see? Will my Lord and His an-gels be wait-ing for me, Be wait-ing, be wait-ing, Will my Lord and His an-gels be wait-ing for me?
(4.) When the cur-tains are lift-ed, Oh, this shall I see, That my Lord and His an-gels are wait-ing for me, Are wait-ing, are wait-ing, That my Lord and His an-gels are wait-ing for me!

Copyright, 1891, by Wm. J. Kirkpatrick.

EVENTIDE. 10s. 209

HENRY F. LYTE.   WILLIAM HENRY MONK.

1. A - bide with me: fast falls the e - ven - tide; The dark-ness
2. Swift to its close ebbs out life's lit - tle day; Earth's joys grow
3. I need Thy pres - ence ev - 'ry pass-ing hour; What but Thy
4. I fear no foe, with Thee at hand to bless; Ills have no

deep - ens; Lord, with me a - bide! When oth - er help - ers
dim, its glo - ries pass a - way; Change and de - cay in
grace can foil the tempter's power? Who, like Thy - self, my
weight, and tears no bit - ter - ness; Where is death's sting? where,

fail, and com-forts flee, Help of the helpless, O a - bide with me!
all a - round I see; O Thou, who changest not, a - bide with me!
guide and stay can be? Thro' cloud and sunshine, Lord, a - bide with me!
grave, Thy vic - to - ry? I tri-umph still, if Thou a - bide with me.

PARTING HYMN. 10s.

Rev. JOHN ELLERTON.   E. J. HOPKINS.

1. Sav - iour! a - gain to Thy dear name we raise With one ac -
2. Grant us Thy peace up - on our homeward way; With Thee be -
3. Grant us Thy peace, Lord! thro' the com - ing night, Turn Thou for
4. Grant us Thy peace throughout our earth - ly life, Our balm in

cord our part - ing hymn of praise: We stand to bless Thee
gan, with Thee shall end, the day; Guard Thou the lips from
us its dark - ness, in - to light; From harm and dan - ger
sor - row and our stay in strife: Then, when Thy voice shall

ere our wor-ship cease. Then, low-ly kneel - ing, wait Thy word of peace.
sin, the hearts from shame, That in this house have called up - on Thy name.
keep Thy chil - dren free For dark and light are both a - like to Thee.
bid our con-flict cease, Call us, O Lord, to Thine e - ter - nal peace.

210 DUKE ST. L. M.

ISAAC WATTS. JOHN HATTON.

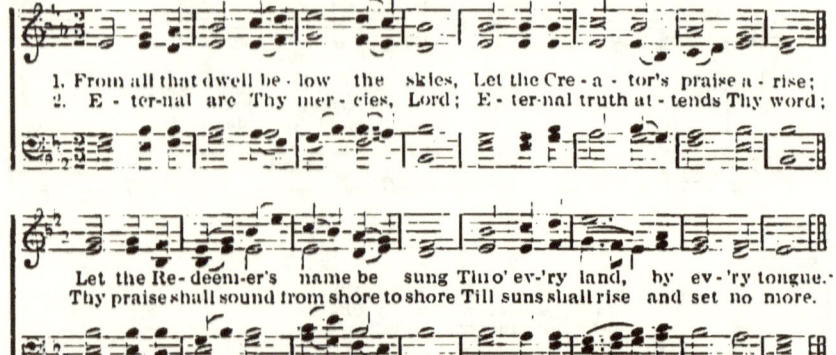

1. From all that dwell be-low the skies, Let the Cre-a-tor's praise a-rise;
2. E-ter-nal are Thy mer-cies, Lord; E-ter-nal truth at-tends Thy word;

Let the Re-deem-er's name be sung Thro' ev-'ry land, by ev-'ry tongue.
Thy praise shall sound from shore to shore Till suns shall rise and set no more.

JESUS SHALL REIGN. L. M.

1 Jesus shall reign where'er the sun
 Does his successive journeys run;
 His kingdom stretch from shore to shore,
 Till moons shall wax and wane no more.

2 From north to south the princes meet
 To pay their homage at His feet;
 While western empires own their Lord,
 And savage tribes attend His word.

3 To Him shall endless prayer be made,
 And endless praises crown His head;
 His name, like sweet perfume, shall rise
 With every morning sacrifice.

4 People and realms, of every tongue,
 Dwell on His love with sweetest song,
 And infant voices shall proclaim
 Their early blessings on His name.
 ISAAC WATTS.

GLORYING IN THE CROSS. L. M.

1 When I survey the wondrous cross
 On which the Prince of glory died,
 My richest gain I count but loss,
 And pour contempt on all my pride.

2 Forbid it, Lord, that I should boast,
 Save in the death of Christ, my God;
 All the vain things that charm me most,
 I sacrifice them to His blood.

3 See, from His head, His hands, His feet,
 Sorrow and love flow mingled down!
 Did e'er such love and sorrow meet?
 Or thorns compose so rich a crown?

4 Were the whole realm of nature mine,
 That were a present far too small:
 Love so amazing, so divine,
 Demands my soul, my life, my all.
 ISAAC WATTS.

HAMBURG. L. M.

Arr. by LOWELL MASON.

LORD, I AM THINE. L. M.

1 Lord, I am Thine, entirely Thine,
 Purchased and saved by blood divine;
 With full consent Thine would I be,
 And own Thy sovereign right in me.

2 Thine would I live, Thine would I die,
 Be Thine through all eternity;
 The vow is past, beyond repeal,
 Now will I set the solemn seal.

3 Here, at that cross where flows the blood
 That bought my guilty soul for God,
 Thee, my new Master, now I call,
 And consecrate to Thee my all.

4 Do Thou assist a feeble worm
 The great engagement to perform;
 Thy grace can full assistance lend,
 And on that grace I dare depend.
 SAMUEL DAVIES.

NOT ASHAMED OF JESUS. L. M.

1 Jesus! and shall it ever be,
 A mortal man ashamed of Thee?
 Ashamed of Thee, whom angels praise,
 Whose glories shine thro' endless days?

2 Ashamed of Jesus! sooner far
 Let evening blush to own a star;
 He sheds the beams of light divine
 O'er this benighted soul of mine.

3 Ashamed of Jesus! just as soon
 Let midnight be ashamed of noon;
 'Tis midnight with my soul till He,
 Bright Morning Star, bid darkness flee.

4 Ashamed of Jesus! that dear Friend,
 On whom my hopes of heaven depend?
 No; when I blush, be this my shame,
 That I no more revere His name.
 JOSEPH GRIGG.

ARLINGTON. C. M. 211

CHARLES WESLEY. THOMAS A. ARNE.

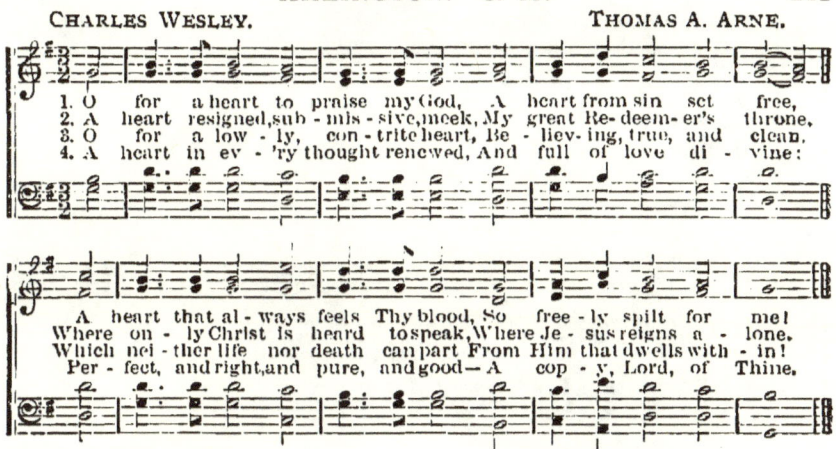

1. O for a heart to praise my God, A heart from sin set free,
   A heart that al - ways feels Thy blood, So free - ly spilt for me!
2. A heart resigned, sub - mis - sive, meek, My great Re - deem - er's throne,
   Where on - ly Christ is heard to speak, Where Je - sus reigns a - lone.
3. O for a low - ly, con - trite heart, Be - liev - ing, true, and clean.
   Which nei - ther life nor death can part From Him that dwells with - in!
4. A heart in ev - 'ry thought renewed, And full of love di - vine:
   Per - fect, and right, and pure, and good— A cop - y, Lord, of Thine.

O FOR A FAITH. C. M.

1 O for a faith that will not shrink,
  Though pressed by ev'ry foe,
  That will not tremble on the brink
  Of any earthly woe!

2 That will not murmur nor complain
  Beneath the chastening rod,
  But, in the hour of grief or pain,
  Will lean upon its God;

3 A faith that shines more bright and clear
  When tempests rage without;
  That when in danger knows no fear,
  In darkness feels no doubt;

4 Lord, give us such a faith as this;
  And then, whate'er may come,
  We'll taste, e'en here, the hallowed bliss
  Of an eternal home.

WILLIAM HILEY BATHURST.

AM I A SOLDIER. C. M.

1 Am I a soldier of the cross,
  A foll'wer of the Lamb,
  And shall I fear to own His cause,
  Or blush to speak His name?

2 Must I be carried to the skies
  On flowery beds of ease,
  While others fought to win the prize,
  And sailed through bloody seas?

3 Are there no foes for me to face?
  Must I not stem the flood?
  Is this vile world a friend to grace,
  To help me on to God?

4 Sure I must fight if I would reign;
  Increase my courage, Lord;
  I'll bear the toil, endure the pain,
  Supported by Thy word.

ISAAC WATTS.

AZMON. C. M.

C. G. GLASER.

FOREVER HERE MY REST. C. M.

1 Forever here my rest shall be,
  Close to Thy bleeding side;
  This all my hope, and all my plea,
  For me the Saviour died.

2 My dying Saviour and my God,
  Fountain for guilt and sin,
  Sprinkle me ever with Thy blood,
  And cleanse and keep me clean.

3 Wash me, and make me Thine own;
  Wash me, and mine Thou art;
  Wash me, but not my feet alone,—
  My hands, my head, my heart.

4 Th' atonement of Thy blood apply,
  Till faith to sight improve;
  Till hope in full fruition die,
  And all my soul be love.

CHARLES WESLEY.

THE DEAREST NAME. C. M.

1 How sweet the name of Jesus sounds
  In a believer's ear!
  It soothes his sorrows, heals his wounds,
  And drives away his fear.

2 It makes the wounded spirit whole,
  And calms the troubled breast;
  'Tis manna to the hungry soul,
  And to the weary, rest.

3 Dear Name, the rock on which I build,
  My shield and hiding-place;
  My never-failing treasury, filled
  With boundless stores of grace.

4 Jesus, my Shepherd, Saviour, Friend,
  My Prophet, Priest, and King;
  My Lord, my Life, my Way, my End,
  Accept the praise I bring!

JOHN NEWTON.

CORONATION. C. M.

E. PERRONET.
OLIVER HOLDEN.

1. All hail the power of Jesus' name! Let angels prostrate fall;
2. Let ev-'ry kindred, ev-'ry tribe, On this ter-res-trial ball,
3. O that, with yonder sacred throng, We at His feet may fall!

Bring forth the roy-al di-a-dem, And crown Him Lord of all;
To Him all maj-es-ty as-cribe, And crown Him Lord of all;
We'll join the ev-er-last-ing song, And crown Him Lord of all;

O FOR A THOUSAND TONGUES.

1 O for a thousand tongues to sing
My great Redeemer's praise!
The glories of my God and King,
The triumphs of His grace!

2 My gracious Master and my God,
Assist me to proclaim,
To spread through all the earth abroad,
The honors of Thy Name.

3 Jesus! the Name that charms our fears,
That bids our sorrows cease;
'Tis music in the sinner's ears,
'Tis life, and health, and peace.

4 He breaks the power of cancell'd sin,
He sets the pris'ner free;
His blood can make the foulest clean;
His blood avail'd for me.

CHARLES WESLEY.

RATHBUN. 8s, 7s.

J. BOWRING.
ITHAMAR CONKEY.

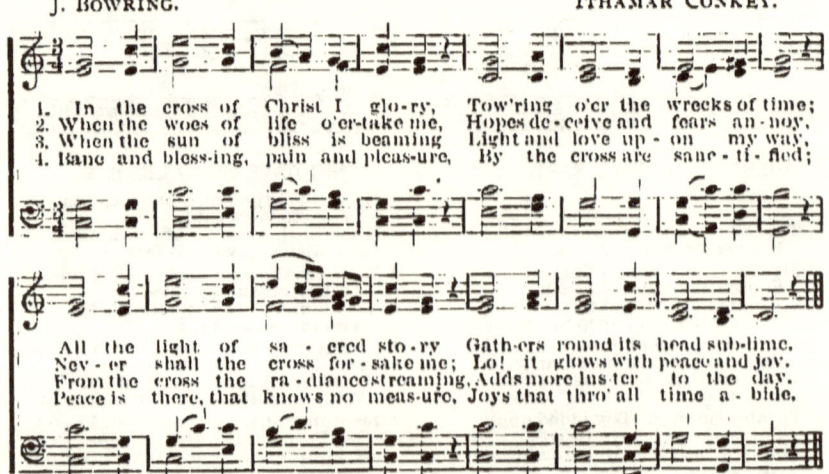

1. In the cross of Christ I glo-ry, Tow'ring o'er the wrecks of time;
2. When the woes of life o'er-take me, Hopes de-ceive and fears an-noy,
3. When the sun of bliss is beaming Light and love up-on my way,
4. Bane and bless-ing, pain and pleas-ure, By the cross are sanc-ti-fied;

All the light of sa-cred sto-ry Gath-ers round its head sub-lime.
Nev-er shall the cross for-sake me; Lo! it glows with peace and joy.
From the cross the ra-diance streaming, Adds more lus-ter to the day.
Peace is there, that knows no meas-ure, Joys that thro' all time a-bide.

DENNIS. S. M. 213

ALBERT MIDLANE.   H. G. NÄGELI.

1. Re-vive thy work, O Lord, Thy might-y arm make bare;
2. Re-vive thy work, O Lord, Cre-ate soul-thirst for Thee;
3. Re-vive thy work, O Lord, Ex-alt Thy pre-cious name;

Speak with the voice that wakes the dead, And make thy peo-ple hear.
And hung'r-ing for the Bread of Life, O may our spir-its be!
And by the Ho-ly Ghost, our love For Thee and Thine in-flame.

BLEST BE THE TIE. S. M.

1 Blest be the tie that binds
   Our hearts in Christian love:
   The fellowship of kindred minds
   Is like to that above.

2 Before our Father's throne
   We pour our ardent prayers;
   Our fears, our hopes, our aims are one,
   Our comforts and our cares.

3 We share our mutual woes,
   Our mutual burdens bear;
   And often for each other flows
   The sympathizing tear.

4 When we asunder part,
   It gives us inward pain;
   But we shall still be joined in heart,
   And hope to meet again.
                     JOHN FAWCETT.

A CHARGE TO KEEP. S. M.

1 A charge to keep I have,
   A God to glorify;
   A never-dying soul to save,
   And fit it for the sky.

2 To serve the present age,
   My calling to fulfill,
   O may it all my powers engage,
   To do my Master's will!

3 Arm me with jealous care,
   As in Thy sight to live;
   And O, thy servant, Lord, prepare
   A strict account to give!

4 Help me to watch and pray,
   And on thyself rely,
   Assured, if I my trust betray,
   I shall forever die.
                     CHAS. WESLEY.

BOYLSTON. S. M.
                        LOWELL MASON.

AND CAN I YET DELAY. S. M.

1 And can I yet delay
   My little all to give?
   To tear my soul from earth away
   For Jesus to receive?

2 Nay, but I yield, I yield!
   I can hold out no more:
   I sink, by dying love compelled,
   And own Thee conqueror!

3 Though late, I all forsake;
   My friends, my all resign;
   Gracious Redeemer, take, O take,
   And seal me ever Thine.

4 Come, and possess me whole,
   Nor hence again remove:
   Settle and fix my wav'ring soul
   With all thy weight of love.
                     CHAS. WESLEY.

EVILS OF INTEMPERANCE. S. M.

1 Mourn for the thousands slain,
   The youthful and the strong;
   Mourn for the wine cup's fearful reign,
   And the deluded throng.

2 Mourn for the ruined soul—
   Eternal life and light
   Lost by the fiery, maddening bowl,
   And turned to hopeless night.

3 Mourn for the lost;—but call,
   Call to the strong, the free;
   Rouse them to shun that dreadful fall,
   And to the refuge flee.

4 Mourn for the lost;—but pray,
   Pray to our God above,
   To break the fell destroyer's sway,
   And show His saving love.

214 MY FAITH LOOKS UP TO THEE.

RAY PALMER. (OLIVET. 6s, 4s.) LOWELL MASON.

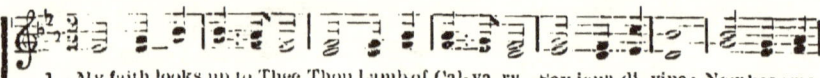

1. My faith looks up to Thee, Thou Lamb of Cal-va-ry. Sav-iour di-vine; Now hear me
2. May Thy rich grace impart Strength to my fainting heart, My zeal inspire! As Thou hast

while I pray Take all my guilt a-way, O let me from this day Be whol-ly thine!
died for me. O may my love to Thee Pure, warm, and changeless be. A living fire!

3 While life's dark maze I tread,
And griefs around me spread,
Be Thou my Guide;
But darkness turn to day,
Wipe sorrow's tears away,
Nor let me ever stray
From Thee aside.

4 When ends life's transient dream,
When death's cold sullen stream
Shall o'er me roll;
Blest Saviour, then, in love,
Fear and distrust remove;
O bear me safe above,
A ransomed soul!

MY COUNTRY! 'TIS OF THEE.

S. F. SMITH. (AMERICA. 6s, 4s.) Ad. HENRY CAREY.

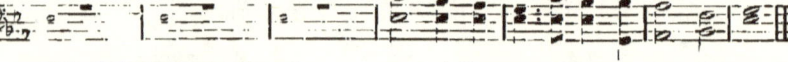

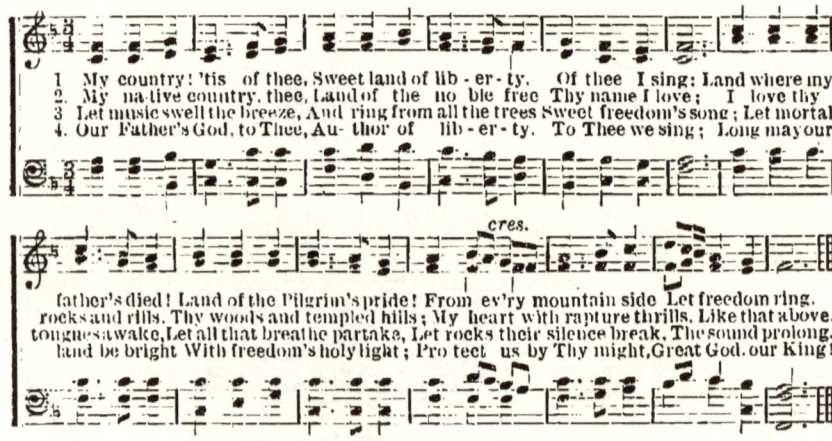

1. My country! 'tis of thee, Sweet land of lib-er-ty, Of thee I sing; Land where my
2. My na-tive country, thee, Land of the no-ble free Thy name I love; I love thy
3. Let music swell the breeze, And ring from all the trees Sweet freedom's song; Let mortal
4. Our Father's God, to Thee, Au-thor of lib-er-ty, To Thee we sing; Long may our

father's died! Land of the Pilgrim's pride! From ev'ry mountain side Let freedom ring.
rocks and rills, Thy woods and templed hills; My heart with rapture thrills, Like that above.
tongues awake, Let all that breathe partake, Let rocks their silence break, The sound prolong.
land be bright With freedom's holy light; Pro-tect us by Thy might, Great God, our King!

COME, THOU ALMIGHTY KING.

C. WESLEY. (ITALIAN HYMN. 6s, 4.) FELICE GIARDINI.

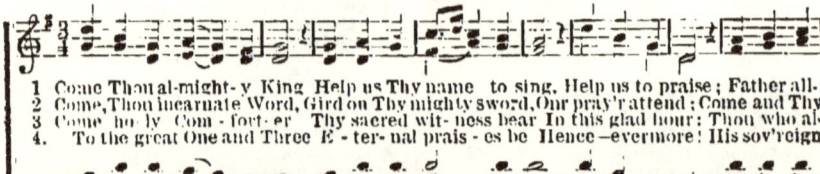

1. Come Thou al-might-y King Help us Thy name to sing, Help us to praise; Father all-
2. Come, Thou incarnate Word, Gird on Thy mighty sword, Our pray'r attend; Come and Thy
3. Come ho-ly Com-fort-er Thy sacred wit-ness bear In this glad hour: Thou who al-
4. To the great One and Three E-ter-nal prais-es be Hence—evermore! His sov'reign

COME, THOU ALMIGHTY KING. Concluded. 215

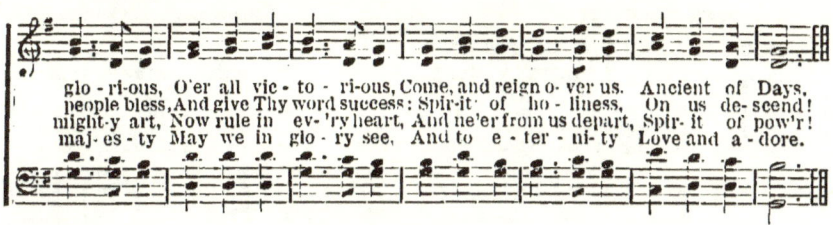

HAPPY DAY.

P. DODDRIDGE.   E. F. RIMBAULT.

2 O happy bond, that seals my vows
   To Him who merits all my love!
  Let cheerful anthems fill His house,
   While to that sacred shrine I move.

3 'Tis done: the great transaction's done!
   I am my Lord's and He is mine;
  He drew me and I followed on.
   Charmed to confess the voice divine.

REVIVE US AGAIN.

WM. P. MACKAY.   J. J. HUSBAND.

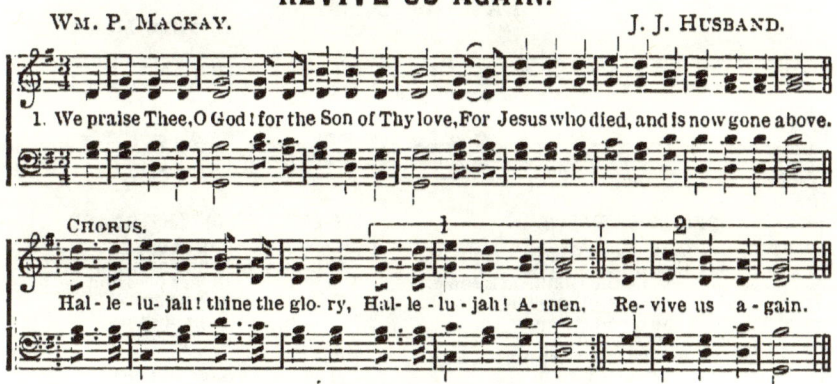

2 We praise Thee, O God! for Thy Spirit of light,
   Who has shown us our Saviour, and scattered our night.
3 All glory and praise to the Lamb that was slain,
   Who has borne all our sins, and has cleansed every stain.
4 All glory and praise to the God of all grace,
   Who has bought us, and sought us, and guided our way.
5 Revive us again; fill each heart with Thy love;
   May each soul be rekindled with fire from above.

ST. THOMAS. S. M.

TIMOTHY DWIGHT.   GEORGE F. HANDEL.

1. I love Thy kingdom, Lord, The house of Thine abode,
The Church our bless'd Redeemer bought With His own precious blood.
2. I love thy Church, O God! Her walls before Thee stand,
Dear as the apple of Thine eye, And graven on Thy hand.
3. For her my tears shall fall, For her my pray'rs ascend;
To her my cares and toils be given, Till toils and cares shall end.

LORD GOD, THE HOLY GHOST.

1 Lord God, the Holy Ghost!
  In this accepted hour,
As on the day of Pentecost,
  Descend in all Thy power.

2 We meet with one accord
  In our appointed place,
And wait the promise of our Lord,
  The Spirit of all grace.

3 Like mighty rushing wind
  Upon the waves beneath,
Move with one impulse every mind;
  One soul, one feeling, breathe.

4 The young, the old, inspire
  With wisdom from above;
And give us hearts and tongues of fire
  To pray, and praise, and love.

          JAMES MONTGOMERY.

GRACE!

1 Grace! 'tis a charming sound!
  Harmonious to my ear!
Heaven with the echo shall resound,
  And all the earth shall hear.

2 Grace first contrived the way
  To save rebellious man;
And all the steps that grace display
  Which drew the wondrous plan.

3 Grace taught my wand'ring feet
  To tread the heavenly road;
And new supplies each hour I meet,
  While pressing on to God.

4 Grace all the work shall crown,
  Through everlasting days;
Its lays in heaven the topmost stone,
  And well deserves the praise.

          P. DODDRIDGE.

LABAN. S. M.

                                        LOWELL MASON.

SPIRIT OF FAITH.

1 Spirit of faith, come down,
  Reveal the things of God;
And make to us the Godhead known,
  And witness with the blood.

2 'Tis thine the blood t' apply,
  And give us eyes to see,
Who did for every sinner die
  Hath surely died for me.

3 O that the world might know
  The all-atoning Lamb!
Spirit of faith, descend, and show
  The virture of His name.

4 The grace which all may find,
  The saving power, impart;
And testify to all mankind,
  And speak in every heart.

          CHARLES WESLEY.

MY SOUL, BE ON THY GUARD.

1 My soul, be on thy guard,
  Ten thousand foes arise,
The hosts of sin are pressing hard
  To draw Thee from the skies.

2 O watch, and fight, and pray,
  The battle ne'er give o'er,
Renew it boldly every day,
  And help divine implore.

3 Ne'er think the vict'ry won,
  Nor lay thine armor down;
The work of faith will not be done,
  Till thou obtain the crown.

4 Fight on, my soul, till death
  Shall bring thee to thy God;
He'll take thee, at thy parting breath,
  To His divine abode.

          GEORGE HEATH.

HORTON. 7s.   217

MARY BARBER DANA.   XAVIER SCHNEIDER.

1. Prince of peace, con-trol my will; Bid this struggling heart be still;
   Bid my fears and doubt-ings cease, Hush my spir-it in-to peace.
2. Thou hast bought me with Thy blood, O-pened wide the gate to God:
   Peace I ask—but peace must be, Lord, in be-ing one with Thee.
3. May Thy will, not mine, be done; May Thy will and mine be one;
   Chase these doubtings from my heart; Now Thy per-fect peace im-part.

HOLY GHOST, WITH LIGHT. 7s.

1 Holy Ghost, with light divine,
 Shine upon this heart of mine;
 Chase the shades of night away,
 Turn my darkness into day.

2 Holy Ghost, with power divine,
 Cleanse this guilty heart of mine;
 Long hath sin, without control,
 Held dominion o'er my soul.

3 Holy Ghost, with joy divine,
 Cheer this saddened heart of mine;
 Bid my many woes depart,
 Heal my wounded, bleeding heart.

4 Holy Spirit, all divine,
 Dwell within this heart of mine;
 Cast down every idol-throne,
 Reign supreme—and reign alone.
          ANDREW REED.

LORD, WE COME. 7s.

1 Lord, we come before Thee now,
 At Thy feet we humbly bow;
 O! do not our suit disdain;
 Shall we seek Thee, Lord, in vain?

2 Lord, on Thee our souls depend;
 In compassion now descend;
 Fill our hearts with Thy rich grace,
 Tune our lips to sing Thy praise.

3 Send some message from Thy word,
 That may joy and peace afford;
 Let Thy Spirit now impart
 Full salvation to each heart.

4 Grant that all may seek and find
 Thee a gracious God, and kind;
 Heal the sick, the captive free;
 Let us all rejoice in Thee.
          WM. HAMMOND.

PLEYEL'S HYMN. 7s.
          IGNACE PLEYEL.

DEPTH OF MERCY. 7s.

1 Depth of mercy? can there be
 Mercy still reserved for me?
 Can my God His wrath forbear?
 Me, the chief of sinners, spare?

2 I have long withstood His grace,
 Long provoked Him to His face;
 Would not hearken to His calls;
 Grieved Him by a thousand falls.

3 Kindled His relentings are;
 Me He now delights to spare;
 Cries, "How shall I give thee up?"
 Lets the lifted thunder drop.

4 There for me the Saviour stands,
 Shows His wounds, and spreads His hands;
 God is love! I know, I feel;
 Jesus weeps and loves me still.
          CHARLES WESLEY.

HOLY BIBLE, BOOK DIVINE. 7s.

1 Holy Bible, book divine,
 Precious treasure, thou art mine;
 Mine, to tell me whence I came;
 Mine to teach me what I am.

2 Mine, to chide me when I rove;
 Mine, to show a Saviour's love;
 Mine art thou to guide my feet;
 Mine to judge, condemn, acquit.

3 Mine to comfort in distress,
 If the Holy Spirit bless;
 Mine, to show by living faith
 Man can triumph over death.

4 Mine to tell of joys to come,
 And the rebel sinner's doom;
 O thou holy book divine,
 Precious treasure, thou art mine.
          JOHN BURTON, SR.

COME THOU FOUNT.

1 Come, Thou Fount of every blessing,
  Tune my heart to sing Thy grace;
  Streams of mercy, never ceasing,
  Call for songs of loudest praise.
  Teach me some melodious sonnet,
  Sung by flaming tongues above;
  Praise the mount, I'm fixed upon it,
  Mount of Thy redeeming love!

2 Here I'll raise mine Ebenezer,
  Hither, by Thy help, I'm come;
  And I hope, by Thy good pleasure,
  Safely to arrive at home.
  Jesus sought me, when a stranger,
  Wand'ring from the fold of God:
  He, to rescue me from danger,
  Interposed His precious blood!

3 O! to grace how great a debtor,
  Daily I'm constrained to be!
  Let Thy goodness, like a fetter,
  Bind my wand'ring heart to Thee!
  Prone to wander, Lord, I feel it,
  Prone to leave the God I love:
  Here's my heart, O take and seal it!
  Seal it for Thy courts above.

  R. ROBINSON.

WHAT A FRIEND.

1 What a friend we have in Jesus,
  All our sins and griefs to bear!
  What a privilege to carry
  Everything to God in prayer!
  O what peace we often forfeit,
  O what needless pain we bear—
  All because we do not carry
  Everything to God in prayer.

2 Have we trials and temptations?
  Is there trouble anywhere?
  We should never be discouraged,
  Take it to the Lord in prayer.
  Can we find a friend so faithful,
  Who will all our sorrows share?
  Jesus knows our every weakness,
  Take it to the Lord in prayer.

3 Are we weak and heavy laden,
  Cumbered with a load of care?
  Precious Saviour, still our refuge,
  Take it to the Lord in prayer.
  Do thy friends despise, forsake thee?
  Take it to the Lord in prayer;
  In His arms He'll take and shield thee,
  Thou wilt find a solace there.

  JOSEPH SCRIVEN.

GREENVILLE. 8s, 7s. D.

COME, YE SINNERS.

1 Come, ye sinners, poor and needy,
  Weak and wounded, sick and sore;
  Jesus ready stands to save you,
  Full of pity, love, and power:
    He is able,
  He is willing, doubt no more.

2 Now, ye needy, come and welcome,
  God's free bounty glorify;
  True belief and true repentance,
  Every grace that brings you nigh,
    Without money,
  Come to Jesus Christ and buy.

3 Let not conscience make you linger,
  Nor of fitness fondly dream;
  All the fitness he requireth
  Is to feel your need of Him:
    This He gives you;
  'Tis the Spirit's glimm'ring beam.

4 Come, ye weary, heavy laden,
  Bruised and mangled by the fall;
  If you tarry till you're better,
  You will never come at all;
    Not the righteous,
  Sinners, Jesus came to call.

  JOSEPH HART.

THE PILGRIM'S GUIDE.

1 Guide me, O Thou great Jehovah,
  Pilgrim through this barren land;
  I am weak, but Thou art mighty;
  Hold me with Thy powerful hand:
    Bread of heaven,
  Feed me till I want no more.

2 Open, now, the crystal fountain,
  Whence the healing waters flow;
  Let the fiery, cloudy pillar
  Lead me all my journey through:
    Strong Deliv'rer,
  Be Thou still my strength and shield.

3 When I tread the verge of Jordan,
  Bid my anxious fears subside;
  Bear me through the swelling current;
  Land me safe on Canaan's side:
    Songs of praises,
  I will ever give to Thee.

  WILLIAM WILLIAMS.

WEBB. 7s, 6s. D. 219

G. J. WEBB.

STAND UP FOR JESUS.

1 Stand up! stand up for Jesus!
  Ye soldiers of the cross;
  Lift high His royal banner,
  It must not suffer loss:
  From vict'ry unto vict'ry
  His army He shall lead,
  Till every foe is vanquished,
  And Christ is Lord indeed.

2 Stand up! stand up for Jesus!
  Stand in His strength alone;
  The arm of flesh will fail you;
  Ye dare not trust your own:
  Put on the gospel armor,
  And, watching unto prayer,
  Where duty calls or danger,
  Be never wanting there.

3 Stand up! stand up for Jesus!
  The strife will not be long;
  This day the noise of battle,
  The next the victor's song:
  To Him that overcometh,
  A crown of life shall be;
  He with the King of Glory
  Shall reign eternally.

GEORGE DUFFIELD, JR.

THE MORNING LIGHT.

1 The morning light is breaking
  The darkness disappears;
  The sons of earth are waking
  To penitential tears:
  Each breeze that sweeps the ocean
  Brings tidings from afar,
  Of nations in commotion,
  Prepared for Zion's war.

2 See heathen nations bending
  Before the God we love,
  And thousand hearts ascending
  In gratitude above;
  While sinners, now confessing,
  The gospel call obey,
  And seek the Saviour's blessing,
  A nation in a day.

3 Blest river of salvation,
  Pursue Thine onward way;
  Flow Thou to every nation,
  Nor in Thy richness stay:
  Stay not till all the lowly
  Triumphant reach their home;
  Stay not till all the holy
  Proclaim, "The Lord is come!"

SAMUEL F. SMITH.

PRAISE GOD.

THOMAS KEN.   OLD HUNDRED. L. M.   LOUIS BOURGEOIS.

INDEX.

Titles in Roman, first lines in Italics.

A.

A Blessing in Prayer,	90
A Charge to Keep,	213
A Shout of Victory,	116
Abide With Me,	209
Alas and Did My Saviour Bleed,	123
All Hail the Power of Jesus'	212
All in Thy Hands,	51
All to Christ I Owe,	103
Am I a Soldier,	211
And Can I Yet Delay,	213
And Shall I Turn Back,	105
Are We Keeping Close to Jesus,	127
Are You Coming to the Feast,	57
Arlington,	211
At My Redeemer's Feet,	86
At the Calling of the Roll,	156
At the Cross,	133
At the Crossing Over Jordan,	158
At the Feet of Jesus,	8
Azmon,	211
A Sinner Though I Am,	87

B.

Beautiful City,	95
Beautiful City of God, The	155
Beautiful Robes,	198
Beautiful Sunshine, The	71
Beautiful Waters of Eden,	188
Beautiful White Clouds,	164
Beyond the Jordan Shore,	45
Blessed Be the Name,	192
Blest Be the Tie,	213
Bought on Calvary,	14
Boylston,	213
Breaking of the Day,	28
Bright Morning Land, The	136
Brother Whence Art Thou Steering,	151

C.

Call to Zion, The	74
Calmly Leaning on My Saviour,	194
Calvary's Stream is Flowing,	202
Christ is Waiting to Save,	32
Cleansed and Redeemed,	106
Cleansing Fountain,	70
Close to Thy Cross, O, Christ,	59
Come, O, Come,	99
Come This Way,	43
Come Thou Almighty King,	214
Come Thou Fount,	218
Come to the Mighty to Save,	118
Come Ye Sinners,	218
Comfort Others,	44
Comforter Has Come, The	204
Coming Home,	67
Coming to the Cross of Jesus,	22
Companionship with Jesus,	176
Consecrated Service,	101
Coronation,	212
Crown Him,	125

D.

Dearest Name, The	211
Dennis,	213
Depth of Mercy,	217
Dreaming of Home,	78
Drifting,	142
Duke, St.	210
Dorology,	219

E.

Entire Consecration,	195
Eventide,	209
Ever the Same,	162
Every Hour for Jesus,	46
Evils of Intemperance,	213

F.

Face the Other Way,	111
Faith, Hope and Love,	35
Follow All the Way,	205
Follow On, Follow On,	131
Forever Here My Rest,	211

G.

Gather Them Into the Fold,	91
Gathered Home,	21
Gathering Sheaves for Jesus,	174
General Roll Call, The	160
Glad All the Day,	30
Gliding Away,	64
Glory to God, Hallelujah,	76
Glorying in the Cross,	210
Good Night,	72
Grace,	216
Gracious Call, The	82
Great Invitation, The	56
Greenville,	218

H.

Hallelujah,	150
Hallelujah, Amen,	193
Hamburg,	210
Happy Day,	215
Happy in the Love of Jesus,	13
Happy Land, The	139
Hark, O Hark,	136
Have You Found the Saviour,	25
He Came to Save Me,	171
He Hideth My Soul,	176
He is Calling,	109
He is My Saviour Divine,	97
He Leads and We Follow,	104
He Saves Me,	122
He Shields from the Storms of Life,	4
Hearest Thou Not,	163
He's Just the Same,	162
He's Mighty to Save,	206
Heaven is My Home,	203
Heavenly Home Across Death's	79
Help Me In, Help Me In,	70
Helper Divine,	26
Hiding, Hiding,	23
Holy Bible, Book Divine,	217
Home to Rest,	137
Holy Ghost With Light,	217
Horton,	217
Hosanna be the Children's Song,	157
How Beautiful to Walk in the	170

I.

I Am Clinging to the Cross,	100
I Am Coming to the Cross of Jesus,	22
I Am Sheltered in Thee,	126
I Have a Wonderful Saviour,	55
I Have Found a Precious Saviour,	148
I Have Peace, Sweet Peace	194
I Love Thy Kingdom, Lord,	216
I Must Tell Jesus	12
I Surrender All,	93
I Will Follow On,	131
I'll Be There,	181
I'm Safe in Jesus,	29
In the Cross of Christ I Glory,	212
In the Hour of Trial,	201
In the Morning, In the Morning,	180
In the Name of Our God,	140
In the Shadow of the Rock,	20
In that Happy Home,	77
It Just Suits Me,	206

J.

Jesus For Me,	199
Jesus Forever the Same,	48
Jesus is Mighty to Save,	10
Jesus, Name of Wondrous Love	83
Jesus Paid it All,	103
Jesus Shall Reign,	210
Jesus the Helper,	26
Jesus Touched My Heart,	165
Joy is Mine, Peace Divine,	114
Just a Little Sunshine,	5
Just a Little While,	24
Just Approach it With a Song,	89
Just as I Am,	175
Just One Touch,	6

K.

Keep Me At the Foot of the Cross,	89
Keep Me Near Thee Blessed Saviour,	88
Keep the Watchfires Burning,	18
King's Highway, The	23

L.

Laban,	216
Lead Kindly Light,	145
Lead Me Saviour,	152
Lead Me to the Rock,	112
Let the Saviour Pilot Thee,	16
Lights of Home, The	164
Like an Army We are Marching,	159
List the Voice,	135
List to the Voice of Jesus,	52
Lo, the Harvest is Nigh,	190
Lo, 'tis Free,	178
Look for the Sunbeams,	115
Look to Jesus,	130
Looking this Way,	161
Lord I Am Thine.	210
Lord I'm Coming Home,	147
Lord, God the Holy Ghost,	216
Lord of Hosts How Lovely, Fair,	173
Lord We Come,	217
Love Divine,	197
Loyalty to the Master.	121

M.

Make Me More Like Jesus,	31
Mear,	177
Meet Me in the Morning,	180
Meet Me There,	192
Missionary Chant,	157
Morning Light, The	219
Music and Love,	107
Must Jesus Bear the Cross,	69
My Bud in Heaven,	138
My Country 'tis of Thee,	214
My Faith Look Up to Thee,	214
My God Shall Supply Your Need,	108
My Saviour,	189
My Soul Be On Thy Guard,	216

N.

Name of Jesus,	66
Nearing My Father's Home.	77
Nettleton,	218
No More Shall We Say Good Bye,	27
Not Ashamed of Jesus,	210

O.

O Blessed Hope,	68
O City of the Living God,	75
O Come the Saviour Calls,	52
O for a Faith,	211
O for a Heart to Praise My God,	211
O for a Thousand Tongues,	212
O God Our Help in Ages Past,	177
O Soul Be Ready,	56
O Glory Land Where We'll Meet,	45
O the Saviour Now is Near,	113
O There is a City,	155
O to Be Like Thee,	11
O What a Resting Place,	128
O I Love the Name of Jesus,	17
One By One We'll Be Gathered,	21
One Thing I Know,	179
Only a Few Brief Years,	191
Out on the Mountain,	135

P.

Palaces of Glory, The	38
Parting Hymn,	209
Pass it On,	202
Perishing Souls,	92
Pilgrim's Guide, The	218
Pleyel's Hymn,	217
Praise God,	219
Praise Him Forever,	84
Praise Ye the Lord,	185
Pressing Onward,	153
Prince of Peace Control My Will,	217

R.

Rathbun,	212
Reap What We've Sown,	80

Redemption,	87
Redemption's Song,	94
Revive Us Again,	215
Ruebush,	173

S.

Saved, O Yes I'm Saved,	87
Saved to the Uttermost,	204
Saviour Pilot Me,	141
Shadow of the Rock, The	20
Sheltered in Thee,	126
Since Jesus Smiled On Me,	9
Sing the Gospel Story,	178
Sitting, Resting, Leaning,	132
Some Sweet Day,	15
Soverign Grace,	3
Sower, The	166
Sowing the Seed,	7
Spirit of Faith,	216
St. Thomas,	216
Stand Up For Jesus,	219
Steersman, the Channel's Rough,	164
Step Out on the Promise of God,	37
Stepping in the Light,	170
Straight Way, The	182
Sunlight,	134
Sunlight All the Way,	110
Sunshine, Sunshine,	71

T.

Take My Life and Let it Be,	195
Tell it to Jesus in Prayer,	62
Tell the Tidings of Salvation,	154
Tell Out With Joy,	154
That Blessed Hope,	117
The Beautiful City of God,	155
The Beautiful Sunshine,	71
The Bright Morning Land,	136
The Call to Zion,	74
The Comforter Has Come,	204
The Dearest Name,	211
The General Roll Call,	160
The Gracious Call,	82
The Great Invitation,	56
The Happy Land,	139
The King's Highway,	23
The Lights of Home,	164
The Morning Light,	219
The Palaces of Glory,	38
The Pilgrim's Guide,	218
The Shadow of the Rock,	20
The Sower,	166
The Straight Way,	182
The True Shepherd,	36
The Wanderers Are Coming Home,	67
The Wanderer's Return,	186
Then Away, Away,	41
Then Forth to Harvest Hasten,	190
There is a Bright and Happy Home	61
There is Cleansing,	54

There is One,	81
There You'll Sing Hallelujah,	207
There's a Heavenly Country,	196
There's a Blessing in Prayer,	90
There's a Friend We Love,	49
There's a Home,	169
Though Your Sins Be Red,	42
'Till My Father Bids Me Come,	96
'Tis at the Feet of Jesus,	8
'Tis so Sweet to Trust in Jesus,	194
Trusting in the Promises,	114
Trusting in Thee,	33

U.

Use Me Dear Saviour,	129

W.

Walking as the Spirit Leads,	47
Walking By the Saviour's Side,	60
Walking in the Sunlight,	34
Wanderers Are Coming Home, The	67
Wanderer's Return, The	186
Washed Whiter Than the Snow,	50
Watch and Pray,	102
We Are Coming,	120
We Have an Anchor,	180
We March to Victory,	41
We Must Work as Well as Play,	85
We Pass This Way But Once,	166
We Shall Walk With Him,	198
We Will Crown Him,	125
We Will Follow, We Will Follow,	104
We Will Set Up Our Banners,	140
Webb,	219
Welcome for Me,	170
We'll Sing His Wonderful Love,	200
We'll Work 'Till Jesus Comes,	73
What a Friend,	218
What Have I Dear Lord to Bring	101
What Rejoicing There Will Be	172
When I Survey Wondrous Cross,	210
When Morning Gilds the Sky,	53
When the Curtains are Lifted,	208
When the Way is So Dark,	149
When We Cross Surging River,	27
Where His Voice is Guiding,	124
Whiter Than the Snow,	42
Who Shall I Send,	184
Who Will Go To-day,	58
Will You Be One,	144
Will You Come Journey With Us,	98
Will You Come to the Feast,	63
Wonderful Salvation,	40
Work and Pray Together,	85
Work for the Master,	146
Worthy the Lamb Who Died,	19

Y.

Ye Christian Heralds, Proclaim,	18

www.ingramcontent.com/pod-product-compliance
Lightning Source LLC
Chambersburg PA
CBHW021844230426
43669CB00008B/1072